This book may be kept
FOURTEEN DAYS

A fine will be charged for each
day the book is kept overtime.

HIGHSMITH 45—226

NEIGHBORS   AT ODDS

ELAINE PASCOE

NEIGHBORS AT↓ODDS

U.S. POLICY IN LATIN AMERICA

› *Franklin Watts* ‹
New York London Toronto Sydney 1990

Map by Joe Le Monnier

Photographs courtesy of:
Bettmann Archive: pp. 19, 38, 61 (bottom);
Culver Pictures: pp. 21, 52, 61 (top), 72;
UPI/Bettmann: pp. 67, 86, 90, 99, 101, 104 (both), 110;
AP/Wide World: pp. 83, 124, 137, 140.

Library of Congress Cataloging-in-Publication Data

Pascoe, Elaine.
Neighbors at odds : U.S. policy in Latin America /
by Elaine Pascoe.
p. cm.
Includes bibliographical references.
Summary: Examines the history of Latin America from the
perspective of its ties with the United States and the conflicts
with the resulting influence of the United States on its fortunes.
ISBN 0-531-10903-8
1. Latin America—Foreign relations—United States—Juvenile
literature. 2. United States—Foreign relations—Latin America—
Juvenile literature. [1. Latin America—Foreign relations—United
States. 2. United States—Foreign relations—Latin America.]
I. Title.
F1418.P36 1990
347.7308—dc20 89-36006 CIP AC

› *Also by Elaine Pascoe* ‹

Racial Prejudice
South Africa: Troubled Land

CONTENTS

NEIGHBORS   AT ODDS

ONE   CLOSE TIES AND CONFLICT

Civil war in Nicaragua . . . "death squad" killings in El Salvador . . . terrorist attacks in Peru . . . drug trafficking in Bolivia. Pick up a newspaper on nearly any day, and you're likely to see stories covering the problems faced by Latin America. The interest is understandable: Latin America (and particularly Central America) has sometimes been called the United States' "backyard." This reference acknowledges the fact that what happens in this region can have a direct effect on the United States—but it also reflects a U.S. tendency to dominate Latin American affairs.

Simple geographical closeness is the most obvious reason for the close link between the United States and the countries of Latin America. Historically, they also share a certain heritage: Like the United States, many of these countries were founded as colonies of European powers and then shook off that rule in revolutions that set demo-

UNITED STATES

Gulf
of Mexico

ATLANTIC
OCEAN

Miami

Havana

Central & South America

● Capital Cities
○ Other Cities

0   1000 Miles

MEXICO

CUBA

HAITI

DOMINICAN REPUBLIC

BELIZE
Belize City
HONDURAS
Tegucigalpa

GUATEMALA
Guatemala
San Salvador
EL SALVADOR
Managua
NICARAGUA
San José
COSTA RICA
PANAMA
Panama City

JAMAICA

PUERTO RICO

Guadaloupe
Dominica
St Lucia
St. Vincent
Barbados

Caracas

Tobago
Trinidad

VENEZUELA

Georgetown
SURINAME
Paramaribo
GUYANA
FRENCH GUIANA
Cayenne

Bogota

COLOMBIA

ECUADOR
Guayaquil
Quito

Manaus

PERU

BRAZIL

Recife

Lima

BOLIVIA
La Paz

Santa Cruz

Brasília

Salvador

PACIFIC
OCEAN

PARAGUAY

Belo Horizonte
São Paulo
Rio de Janeiro

CHILE

Asunción

ARGENTINA

Córdoba

URUGUAY

Santiago

Buenos Aires
Montevideo

Bahía Blanca

cratic government as their goal. Latin America is also one of the United States' most important trading partners and the site of much U.S. investment. And in recent years, another factor has drawn the United States closer to Latin America: immigration. As growing numbers of immigrants from Mexico, Puerto Rico, the Caribbean, and Central America have entered the United States, events in Latin America have taken on increasing importance.

Yet, for all the ties that draw them together, the history of relations between the United States and Latin American countries has often been one of friction and misunderstanding.

Since the early 1800s, the United States has believed strongly that its national security is linked to the stability of Latin America, and it has vigorously opposed the influence of other foreign powers there. As the United States has achieved superpower status in the twentieth century, it has tended to see its relationship with Latin America in broader terms. Through diplomacy and more forceful measures, the United States has sought to maintain a sphere of influence in Latin America, keeping the countries of the region politically and economically aligned with its interests.

To some people, the U.S. approach simply reflects the facts of the situation: As the most powerful political and economic force in the region, they say, it is inevitable that the United States will take a dominant role. But U.S. policies have often bred resentment in Latin America and criticism abroad. And these policies have been no less controversial at home. The 1980s alone have seen heated debates over armed intervention in the Caribbean island of Grenada, support of rebels in Nicaragua, devastating economic pressures brought by the United States on Panama, and support of Latin American regimes accused of political repression and violations of human rights. At the same time, however, the United States has poured vast amounts of aid into Latin America and has used its influence to reduce some of the more flagrant human rights abuses—political kidnappings, torture, murder—that plague the region.

Thus, Uncle Sam presents two faces in the region: the kindly uncle, offering help to less fortunate relatives, and the domineering uncle, willing to ride roughshod over their rights. In fact, the situation is far more complex than either characterization suggests. For one thing, U.S. influence in Latin America has been on the decline in recent years. Economically, Latin America has broadened its range of trading partners, and Japan and other countries have increased their share of investment in the region. Politically, Latin American countries have more and more sought to steer an independent course, even when this has brought them into open disagreement with the United States. The Soviet Union has made its presence felt in Cuba and Nicaragua, and some analysts see the Soviets as the guiding force behind many of the region's revolutionary movements.

The United States remains the most important outside influence on Latin America. But many analysts see a growing need for a reassessment of U.S. foreign policy in the region. Too often, they say, past policies have been based on ignorance of and misunderstandings about the region. North

Americans tend to view their neighbors to the south in simplistic—and often negative—terms. Stereotypes abound: The region is impoverished and politically unstable, a land of harsh dictators and Communist revolutionaries; its people are backward, lazy, and emotional.

In fact, Latin America is a region of enormous diversity, in politics and geography, heritage and aspirations. It covers a vast area, two and a half times that of the United States, and includes some twenty-five countries, ranging from Brazil (which itself is larger than the continental United States) to the tiny island states of the Caribbean. While these countries have much in common, they have differences as well—in history, social structure, natural wealth, economic development, and political orientation.

Above all, the region is rapidly changing and evolving. In many countries, economic growth and modernization are bringing increasing pressures for political and social reform. To some analysts, this is a key factor in the confusion and controversy over U.S. Latin American policy. Too often, they say, the United States has misinterpreted pressure for reform as a tilt toward Communism and has blocked change, maintaining the appearance of stability but increasing friction and resentment.

The following chapters will take a closer look at some of the basic differences between the United States and Latin America and will trace the history of U.S. foreign policy in the region, from the early 1800s to current times. We can't hope to cover every incident or twist in the history of U.S.–Latin American relations or to provide an in-depth analysis of U.S. policy. But examining the major trends that have shaped past U.S. relations with the region will help shed light on the problems of today—and perhaps suggest a better course of action for the future.

TWO   DIFFERENT CULTURES

The term "Latin America" itself points to one major difference between this region and the United States: language. With a few exceptions in the Caribbean area, where Britain and France made their influence felt, Latin America was colonized by two great rivals, Spain and Portugal. As a result, Spanish and Portuguese—two Romance, or Latin-based, languages—are the dominant tongues in the region. The Portuguese established their rule on the eastern coast of South America, and today Portuguese is spoken in Brazil. The rest of South America, most of Central America and the Caribbean, and Mexico fell under Spanish rule, and as a result Spanish is spoken throughout these areas.

But language is only one of the differences between Latin America and its neighbors to the north. As Spanish and Portuguese colonies, the countries that today form Latin America developed socially and culturally along lines that were quite different from those in the United States and Canada. To a large extent, the social structures and cultural traditions formed in colonial times survived independence, and this heritage has influenced many of the problems faced by Latin America.

Colonial Rule ›

Until the arrival of Europeans, Latin America was inhabited by Indians who were divided into many different language and culture groups. They included some of the most advanced Indian civilizations on record: the Aztec and Maya, in the area that is now Mexico and Central America, and the Inca, in the region new formed by Peru, Ecuador, and Bolivia. These people were builders of cities, roads, and temples, and they made great advances in mathematics, engineering, astronomy, medicine, and art. For the most part, their societies were marked by a strong central government and a rigid hierarchy, with priests and emperors at the top and vassals and slaves at the bottom.

The arrival of Christopher Columbus in the Caribbean in 1492 signaled the beginning of the end for these cultures. After 1521, when the Aztecs were defeated by Spanish forces under Hernán Cortés, the entire region fell rapidly under European domination. Central America was firmly under Spanish control by 1525; ten years later, the Spanish completed their conquest of the Incas. By the mid-1500s, they had extended their claim north into the region that would later become the western United States and south to the tip of South America, claiming most of the western territory.

*The Temple of Quetzalcoatl in Mexico illustrates
the building talent of the advanced Indian
civilizations that inhabited that region.*

By treaty, the Spanish agreed that eastern South America would fall to Portugal, and the Portuguese sea captain Pedro Álvares Cabral formally laid claim to this region in 1500.

The Indian population at the time of European "discovery" is unknown, but some estimates put it as high as 100 million. The Spanish forces, particularly at the outset of the conquest, numbered in the hundreds; but the Spanish were able to impose their rule on the Indians with the help of several key factors. One was equipment: horses and guns. Another was opportune timing: Both the Incas and the Aztecs were faced with internal divisions and unrest in their empires when the Spanish arrived. The Aztecs were undone by two additional factors—they initially believed that Cortés was a god, Quetzalcoatl, and so allowed the Spanish invaders to get the jump on them. And contact with Europeans brought a raging outbreak of smallpox to the Indians; with no natural immunity to the disease, their population was decimated.

Conquest brought hoards of Indian gold and silver to the Spanish, and Spanish settlers soon arrived in the hope of sharing in the riches of the New World. They developed mining and agriculture, and designed and built new cities. For these efforts, labor was needed—and a ready source of labor was at hand among the Indians. Despite the

The Aztecs thought Cortés was the god Quetzalcoatl, so they did not initially fight him and his men.

fact that they made up the overwhelming majority of the population, and regardless of their former status, all Indians were now at the bottom of the social order.

For a time, the Indians became virtual slaves of their conquerors. By an edict issued by the Spanish Queen Isabella, they were required to work for the colonists; and each colonist was allotted a certain number of Indian laborers under a system known as *encomienda* ("entrustment"). Mistreatment was rampant, and in 1542 the Spanish crown issued new laws that brought the Indians under the direct control of the crown in an effort to protect them. In practice, though, the change meant little for the Indians—their assignments as laborers were temporary rather than permanent, but they still had no choice in the matter.

Land that the Indians had once controlled was divided up among the settlers. The Spanish crown granted enormous tracts of land to the early colonists, and individual holdings grew steadily larger as neighbors bought out neighbors. In some areas, *haciendas* (ranches) grew to a million acres or more. With such enormous tracts at their disposal, the Spanish often converted fertile farmland to pasture for raising livestock or left it fallow. Landowners, meanwhile, became virtual princes within their domains. Anyone who lived on a *hacienda* was under the authority of the landowner, who controlled all trade with the outside world and was free to use force to ensure his tenants' compliance. This situation evolved into a system of peonage, in which landless laborers were bound in service to the landholders.

As they lost their freedom and their land, the Indians also saw their culture and traditions undermined. Where they could, they evaded their conquerers by retreating into remote interior areas. Theirs became a second culture, hidden beneath the overlay of Spanish rule. Meanwhile, disease—smallpox, measles, and influenza, to all of which the Indians lacked immunity—continued to take its toll, particularly among men. In some areas, the Indian population decreased by 90 percent by the early 1600s. Casualties were particularly high among Indians who were taken to work the new lowland, coastal plantations that were developing in many areas; they were ill suited to the climate and the work.

As a result, the Spanish and Portuguese soon found themselves faced with a problem they had not anticipated: a labor shortage. Their solution, particularly in the Caribbean and in the tropical lowland areas, was to bring in black slaves from Africa. In their three centuries of rule, the Spanish imported more than 1.5 million black slaves. In eastern South America, where the Indian population was smaller, less settled, and less advanced than it was in most of the Spanish holdings, the Portuguese imported more than twice that number of black slaves to work the enormous sugar plantations they were developing along the coast. By the early 1800s, blacks made up almost half the population of this area.

The arrival of the Africans added another set of cultural traditions to the new society. On the whole, the lines between the races were less firmly drawn in Latin America than they were in North

America, where whites, blacks, and Indians remained separate groups. Among the early colonists in some areas, men outnumbered women by as much as seven to one; and thus liaisons between Spanish men and Indian women became commonplace. Their mixed-race descendants, known as *mestizos*, became a growing segment of the population. With blacks as with the Indians, racial blending took place. Mulattoes, the descendants of whites and blacks, joined a lively mix that included whites, Indians, *mestizos*, black slaves, and blacks who had escaped slavery or been granted their freedom. While legal marriages between whites and blacks or whites and Indians were rare, racial mixing continued with whites marrying *mestizos* or mulattoes, *mestizos* marrying Indians, mulattoes marrying blacks, and so on. Along with this came a blending of cultural traditions.

All the same, there were clear levels of status in the colonial society, and where a person stood depended on his or her origin and occupation as well as race. Among whites, for example, there was friction between *peninsulares* (those who were born in Spain) and *criollos* or creoles (those who were born in the colonies). Similar divisions and rivalries developed between merchants and landowners.

This mixed and varied population lived under a system of government that was highly autocratic. In England, the Magna Carta and a rambunctious Parliament had weakened the authority of the king and introduced the idea that the power of government rested ultimately with the people. Spain and Portugal had no such tradition. In the New World as in Europe, the Spanish and Portuguese monarchs were the ultimate authorities in their territories, ruling by divine right.

Both countries, but Spain in particular, set up elaborate, multitiered bureaucracies to keep a firm economic and social grip on their holdings. The territories were split into separate areas for the purposes of government. By the end of the 1700s, Spain had set up four viceroyalties in the New World: New Spain (Mexico and northern Central America), New Grenada (the rest of Central America and the northern part of South America, including Venezuela and Colombia), Peru (including present-day Chile), and La Plata (including present-day Argentina and other territory south of Brazil). Portugal had two states in the area that would eventually become Brazil, and it added new territory as it explored the dense Amazon jungles. Both the Spanish and Portuguese areas were further divided into captaincies and similar divisions, each with its own local governor. The fact that the colonies were so distant from the mother countries gave the viceroys and other regional officials considerable leeway, and they often tended to set their own rules.

Aiding the rulers in keeping this system running smoothly were two important elements in colonial Latin American society: the military and the Roman Catholic Church. The military was important from the beginning, particularly in Spanish America, where the conquerors were faced with the task of keeping a large and established Indian population under control. It evolved into an elite group, closely involved in the government. In many areas, local militias formed by landowners helped the regular army maintain order. (In North America, by contrast, colonists made few attempts to subjugate the Indians. The military's role was to push the Indians back and defend the colonists from their counterattacks; it took little part in the day-to-day life of the colonies.)

The Church's role presented another sharp contrast with North America. Unlike religious groups in the United States, where religious tolerance and separation of church and state were founding principles, the Church in Latin America functioned almost as an arm of government. This role followed logically from the belief that the ultimate authority of the government flowed through the monarch from God, rather than from the people. The Church saw a mission in the New World: the conversion of the Indians. To accomplish that goal, it established a system of missions and holdings throughout the territories. The missions brought European learning to the Indians, but they also helped extend state control and impose censorship—matters that were enforced through the harsh measures of the Inquisition. Meanwhile, the missions enabled the Church to amass enormous wealth and power, until it became almost a state within a state.

Economically, the Spanish and Portuguese colonies were intended to serve as milk cows for the mother countries. Exports of gold and silver, hardwoods, and other natural resources flowed from them to Europe. Agriculture was focused on single crops for export, such as sugar (and later coffee) in Brazil. Trade was strictly controlled. To ensure that the colonial powers would get the full benefit of the continent's natural wealth, the colonies were not allowed to trade with other countries. And the development of industries that would make the colonies self-sufficient was discouraged; in Brazil, for example, a royal decree banned all industry in 1785. The New World was needed not only as a source of raw materials but also as a market for finished goods produced by the mother countries.

With a few notable exceptions—a serious uprising among the Incas in 1780, widespread protests the following year over taxes in the Spanish colony of New Grenada, a revolt in Portuguese Bahia in 1798—Spanish and Portuguese rule continued untroubled for some three hundred years. Its legacy was a society with certain distinct features that set Latin America apart from North America. As noted, there was greater racial and cultural variety, but society was strictly organized by status. Land and wealth were concentrated in the hands of the few, while the bulk of the population was made up of landless laborers who lived in poverty. The Church and the military were seen as natural sources of authority, and governmental authority on the whole was viewed as something that was handed down from above and accepted by the people, rather than originating with their consent. The economy was based on exports of raw materials and cash crops to limited overseas markets, so that Latin America lagged behind Europe in the development of industry, technology, and a skilled labor force.

Toward Independence ›

This society didn't exist in a vacuum, of course. Other European powers increasingly came on the scene: France, Britain, and the Netherlands established colonies in the Caribbean and along the eastern coast of the mainland. And in the 1700s, many members of the creole elite were educated in Europe. There, as they read works by Smith, Locke, Rousseau, and other authors of the Enlightenment, they encountered the same ideas that influenced the American Revolution. It was not too difficult to sneak copies of these works past the Spanish censors, and so they were read by the elite in the colonies as well. As a result, many Latin Americans sympathized with the American and French revolutions and the ideals they stood for. By the early 1800s, the works of Thomas Jefferson, Benjamin Franklin, Thomas Paine, and other revolutionary leaders were also well known among the educated classes to the south.

Latin America's own push for independence came in the early 1800s. In a series of revolts, most of the Spanish possessions gained their freedom between 1804 and 1824, while Brazil underwent a more gradual transition that culminated in full independence in 1823. But ideas were not the only driving force for freedom in Latin America. While most of the revolutionary leaders espoused the ideals of the Enlightenment, economic and political concerns were foremost in many peoples' minds. Nor were the Latin American revolutions broad-based, popular movements that involved people from all walks of life. By and large, these were revolutions of, by, and for the elite.

In Spanish America, friction between creoles and *peninsulares* was a major factor. In the mid- to late 1700s, Spain had reorganized the colonial system to give the crown more direct control. Creoles were in many cases pushed out of government and replaced by officials from the mother country. While creoles were able to exercise some authority in local town councils, or *cabildos*, they were upset by the loss of power and prestige.

The Spanish crown also acted against the Church and the military, seeing them as potential rivals for control. The wealthy and powerful Jesuit order was expelled from Spanish America in 1767, and its holdings were auctioned off. To counter the military, the crown set up a system of colonial militias. By the end of the century, these largely creole forces vastly outnumbered regular Spanish troops in the New World. Under pressure from the creoles, the Spanish also loosened some trade restrictions. But the economic benefits this produced were not enough to offset the creoles' growing dissatisfaction.

Thus, the Spanish crown succeeded in organizing and arming the creoles at a time when they were increasingly unhappy with Spanish rule and increasingly influenced by revolutionary ideas. Still, the spark that ignited rebellion in Latin America was struck by an event in Europe: Napoleon's invasion of the Iberian Peninsula in the early 1800s.

The French dictator occupied Portugal in 1807, forcing the Portuguese royal family to flee to Brazil. With Brazil as his base, and the mother country—for all intents and purposes—out of the picture, the Portuguese ruler Dom João VI brought vast changes to the colony, opening trade with other countries and making a start on industrial development. After the French were driven out of Portugal and Dom João returned to Lisbon in 1821, his son Dom Pedro remained behind as prince regent. Soon Portugal was calling for its trade monopoly and political authority to be reestablished—but the Brazilian elite, who had benefited enormously from the changes, would have none of it. Under pressure from this group, Dom Pedro refused to return to Portugal or to assent to the changes, and in 1822 he declared Brazil free of Portuguese control.

Although Brazil had to put down a pro-Portuguese revolt in Bahia (which it did in 1823), independence was gained without much bloodshed—by this time, the former colony was stronger than the mother country. But if independence came painlessly, it brought no great changes in most people's way of life. The chief difference was that in place of the Portuguese crown, Brazil now had an independent monarch of its own. It remained a monarchy until 1889.

In most of Spanish America, the transition to independence was not so smooth. There, a series of events served as catalysts for revolution. Napoleon captured Madrid in 1808 and put his brother Joseph on the throne in place of the Spanish king Ferdinand VII. Ferdinand's supporters, meanwhile, set up a junta in Seville to rule in his name. *Cabildos* in Buenos Aires and Venezuela met and decided to set up similar juntas, loyal to Ferdinand.

Among the leaders of the Venezuelan group was Simón Bolívar, who, like most of the other members of the *cabildos*, was from a wealthy creole family. Bolívar had been educated abroad, and his vision for Latin America went further than that of many of his compatriots: He wanted independence, under a republican form of government. In

1811, he won the support of the council that governed Venezuela, and independence was declared. But it was not so easily achieved—the Seville junta sent troops to put down the revolt. Bolívar's fortunes seesawed up and down. Finally, in 1819, he succeeded in gaining control of Venezuela. He then turned south with his forces, hoping to unite Spanish America as one independent state.

Events in Argentina followed a similar course, under the leadership of José de San Martín. Like Bolívar, San Martín was a member of the elite. By 1817, he had gained control of most of Argentina. Then, in a daring move, he led his army across the Andes to stage a surprise attack on Spanish forces in Chile. As Bolívar's forces moved south, San Martín's moved north, up South America's western coast.

But both leaders soon found that their goal of independence was not universally shared. Particularly after Ferdinand returned to the Spanish throne in 1814, many creoles saw less purpose in independence; indeed, a change in the status quo would threaten their position. Then, in 1820, came a turn of events that renewed the independence movement: Ferdinand suddenly endorsed a group of liberalizing changes that had first been proposed by the Seville junta. Among them were a shift in power away from the monarchy and toward parliament, and strict limits to the power of the Church, including an end to the Inquisition.

Many members of the elite in Spanish America saw these changes as a greater threat to their position than independence; they opted for the latter. San Martín declared Peru independent in

1821, the same year that Bolívar united Venezuela, Colombia, and Ecuador into the new state of Gran Colombia. Three years later, rebel troops under General Antonio José de Sucre delivered a final and decisive defeat to Spanish forces at the Battle of Ayacucho in Peru.

Bolívar's early vision of a united and democratic Latin America was not widely shared, however. Each region wanted to set up as its own independent state. Gran Colombia fell apart. San Martín reportedly favored a monarchy and resigned his offices when the proposal was not well received. Bolívar himself acknowledged that full democracy might be an unreachable goal for these new states.

In Bolivia, the state named for him, he was named president for life. Elsewhere, the tendency was for the newly independent Latin American countries to go through a series of unstable regimes, each headed by a strong man, or *caudillo*. Rarely did these changes in government have any direct effect on the common people. The existing social structure remained in place, with the creole elite replacing the Spanish.

One of the few true popular uprisings of this time took place in Mexico, where a priest named Miguel Hidalgo y Costilla led a force of mixed-race and Indian rebels against the Spanish. When the revolt broke out in 1810, Hidalgo scored a series of victories, but on the outskirts of Mexico City he inexplicably pulled back. Early the next year, Hidalgo was captured and executed. Others took over the fight, but the Spanish gradually gained the upper hand.

In the end, it was the elite that took Mexico away from Spain. In 1822, alarmed over the liberal changes adopted by King Ferdinand, the Spanish commander Agustín de Iturbide switched sides and struck a pact with the rebels. He then marched on Mexico City, declared independence, and set himself up as emperor. Central Americans, equally alarmed by the changes in Spain, threw their lot in with his and joined the empire. But Iturbide's empire was short-lived—faced with revolts by both elite and popular leaders, he abdicated in 1823. Central America split away from Mexico. Mexico would face a long struggle between conservatives who wanted to maintain the status quo and liberals who pressed for reform.

As elsewhere in Latin America, independence had not brought significant changes to society. Wealth and power in the new Latin American countries remained in the hands of landowners and merchants. Indeed, in areas where the fighting was greatest, the Latin American economies—still dependent on the export of a few products—were disrupted, and poverty increased. Economic problems in turn contributed to weakness and instability in government. Another legacy of the revolutionary movements was an increase in the power of the military. As regional and factional fighting continued to disrupt the new countries, strong armies and militias became essential. The *caudillos* who took power in many areas were often soldiers.

The revolutionary movements had introduced new elements to the Latin American tradition, however. The leaders of these movements—Bolívar, San Martín, de Sucre, Hidalgo, and others such as Bernardo O'Higgins, the liberator of Chile; Manuel Belgrano, the Argentine general; and José Bonifácio de Andrada e Silva, who worked for independence and democracy in Brazil—were glorified. Along with that glorification came a general admiration for the democratic ideals many of the leaders espoused, even if those ideals were seldom put into practice. In some areas, including Mexico and Paraguay, new ideas—land reform, social and racial equality—had at least been introduced. Legal barriers between races were on the whole abolished (although slavery continued in Brazil into the late 1800s). While *mestizos* and other groups remained economically and socially disadvantaged, some *mestizos* found their first real opportunity to advance in the military, where ability outweighed skin color and family name.

This, then, was the nature of the society that the United States saw when it turned its eyes south and, in the early 1800s, began to formulate a policy toward Latin America.

THREE   THE MONROE DOCTRINE

The Latin American independence movements developed in a time of international turmoil. The major European powers were embroiled in the Napoleonic wars until 1815, when the Battle of Waterloo put an end to Napoleon's ambitions. The United States—itself just thirty-five years from independence—was struggling to establish itself on a continent that was dominated by those powers, and its position colored its outlook toward the emerging Latin American republics. To the government of the United States, national security was the paramount concern at this time. The country was small, new, and essentially weak—it consisted of a band of territory along the eastern coast of North America, and the rest of the hemisphere was in the strong hands of Britain, France, Spain, and the other European powers.

The first question was a basic one: whether to recognize the new Latin American states. When

Simón Bolívar declared the independence of Venezuela from Spain in 1811, the United States was on the brink of war with Britain. The War of 1812 would occupy the country's attention until the end of 1814, when the Treaty of Ghent was signed. But even then, the U.S. government did not rush to support the revolutionary fever that was sweeping through the hemisphere to the south.

This was not for lack of sympathy. United States public opinion was solidly behind the Latin American revolutions—not only might independent Latin American states prove useful allies against the colonial ambitions of the Europeans, but the leaders of the revolutions expressed ideals that echoed those of the American Revolution. People in the United States were flattered by what they saw as emulation. Several U.S. ports became bases for privateers who supported the rebels, prompting Congress to officially assert U.S. neutrality in 1818. Public pressure for the U.S. government to recognize the new republics to the south was growing. The famous orator Henry Clay spoke for it on the floor of the House of Representatives, referring to "the glorious spectacle of eighteen millions of people, struggling to burst their chains and to be free."[1]

But for the government, recognizing the new republics presented something of a dilemma. Too prompt and enthusiastic a response to the revolutions might spark an attack from Spain. Having so recently been in conflict with Britain, the United States was not keen to begin another war. Moreover, in order to stand up to Europe, the United States would have had to be stronger. With the exception of its fight with Britain, the United States in the early 1800s hoped to avoid conflict while it gradually grew in strength.

One way to build that strength was through territorial expansion. As Napoleon's armies redrew the map of Europe, the fluctuating fortunes of the European colonial powers had already created openings for the United States.

Expansion Begins ›

The Louisiana Purchase in 1803 had been the first windfall. Napoleon had once dreamed of vast New World holdings, but his army had been bogged down by yellow fever and by a bloody slave revolt in the Caribbean. With matters in Europe more pressing, he had abandoned the idea and sold New Orleans and a vast tract of land west of the Mississippi River to the United States. There were questions about the legality of the transfer—at the time of the purchase, the territory had only recently been transferred from Spain to France, and Spanish troops were still in possession. The Spanish were outraged—they did not consider Louisiana Napoleon's to sell. But, faced with the turmoil of war at home and growing unrest in its colonies, Spain was unwilling to fight to keep the territory.

To the United States, the vast amount of land included in the purchase was a bonus (it doubled the size of the country in one blow). The government was not even clear on the exact boundaries of the territory—whether, for example, it might include parts of Florida and Texas. Access to the Gulf of Mexico was the most important benefit of the purchase; in a time when trade depended almost entirely on ocean shipping, the acquisition of

Monroe and Livingstone negotiate the Louisiana Purchase with France's Tallyrand in 1803. The purchase doubled the size of the young United States.

a Gulf port (especially one at the mouth of the Mississippi) in effect gave the country a back door. Soon the United States looked to extend its foothold on the Gulf, moving east into the Spanish territory of Florida.

The spirit of revolution in Latin America helped provide a wedge. With the encouragement of the U.S. government, a group of American settlers in West Florida took a step that would later be repeated on a much larger scale in Texas: They rebelled against Spanish rule, set up their own tiny republic, and then joined the United States. In 1813, U.S. annexation of West Florida was cemented when the last Spanish troops were evicted from Mobile. But East Florida—the strategic peninsula that dominates the Gulf of Mexico—was still in Spanish hands.

The United States hoped to gain this territory through negotiation with Spain (a fact that made the government even less willing to offend the Spanish by supporting the revolutions in their other territories). But negotiations made little headway until 1818. By that time, the Spanish had been forced to withdraw troops from Florida to fight the revolutions in South America. General Andrew Jackson, ostensibly in hot pursuit of Indian raiders, crossed into the territory and rapidly seized every major port except St. Augustine. The action was unauthorized, and the United States split over it, with some people condemning it and others attempting to justify it. But, justified or not, U.S. control of Florida was a *fait accompli.* Spain ceded the territory in 1819, in exchange for a U.S. promise to stay out of Texas and the renunciation of some $5 million in claims that U.S. citizens had brought against the Spanish.

With Mexico in turmoil and the United States firmly established in Louisiana and Florida, the Gulf was no longer a Spanish lake. In fact, the Spanish were being routed throughout the hemisphere. But the United States continued to hold off in recognizing the Latin American republics for more than a year, while political unrest in Spain caused the Spanish to delay ratification of the treaty ceding Florida. Finally, in December 1823, President James Monroe recommended the step to Congress.

The Monroe Doctrine ›

The acquisition of Gulf ports put the United States in a far stronger position than it had been at the start of the 1800s. But the 1820s presented new threats to national security. With the end of the Napoleonic wars in Europe, hereditary monarchs had returned to their thrones, intent on restoring order and stamping out a rash of revolutions that had broken out in Europe in the aftermath of the wars.

In 1815, Austria, Prussia, England, and Russia formed the Quadruple Alliance; after the French monarchy was restored and France joined the alliance in 1818, it became generally known as the Quintuple, or Holy, Alliance. One of the stated goals of the group was an end to democracy. England, finding its interests and inclinations increasingly different from the rest of the countries, gradually drifted away. But the others moved to crush revolts in Portugal and Naples. When a revolution once again unseated Ferdinand VII, a

French army invaded Spain in 1823 and restored him to his throne.

Having reestablished order at home, the European monarchs turned their eyes overseas, hoping to reassert control over their empires. Speculation was high that the group planned a joint attack on Latin America, to reclaim Spain's lost territories. This alarmed the United States—Spain alone might not be able to topple the fledgling Latin American states, but how would they stand up to the combined strength of Europe? And if the Alliance succeeded in securing Latin America, might the European group—with its hatred of democracy—attack the United States?

The concerns were economic as well as political. Once they were freed of the restrictions imposed by Spain and Portugal, the Latin American states had begun to trade heavily with England and the United States. England, with its vast naval and merchant fleets, took the bulk of the trade—a factor that helped move it away from the other members of the Alliance. But the U.S. share was growing. By the early 1820s, Latin America was receiving about 30 percent of U.S. exports. If Spain regained control of the region, this booming market would be closed.

The United States was threatened not only to the south but also to the northwest. In 1821, Russia, which controlled Alaska and had established trading posts down the West Coast into California (then part of Mexico), claimed sovereignty over the seas as far south as the 51st parallel. This seemed to indicate that the Russians were preparing to extend their control into the Oregon region, which was already claimed by both Britain and the United

States. If they succeeded, and if Spain succeeded in regaining control over Mexico, the United States would find itself hemmed in on the west by the countries of the Alliance.

By late 1823, President James Monroe was becoming increasingly worried, particularly over the threat to Latin America. John Quincy Adams, his secretary of state, wrote in his memoirs that the president was "alarmed, far beyond anything that I could have conceived possible, with the fear that the Holy Alliance are about to restore immediately all South America to Spain." Adams himself was less concerned. He felt that unrest in Europe would continue to occupy the Alliance powers and make the threat of immediate action in Latin America less likely. But even he acknowledged that the Alliance posed "a fearful question."[2]

The outgrowth of Monroe's concern was a statement, made on December 2, 1823, that was to become known as the Monroe Doctrine and would serve as the foundation of U.S. policy toward Latin America for years to come. The policy was outlined in two separate passages in Monroe's annual address to Congress. In the first, after alluding to Russia's claims in the Northwest, the president stated:

> *The American continents, by the free and independent condition which they have assumed and maintain, are henceforth not to be considered as subjects for future colonization by any European powers.*

The second passage was directed to the problem of Latin America. After noting that the monarchical system favored by members of the Alliance was "essentially different" from America's political system, Monroe said:

> *We owe it, therefore, to candor and to the amicable relations existing between the United States and those powers to declare that we should consider any attempt on their part to extend their system to any portion of this hemisphere as dangerous to our peace and safety. With the existing colonies or dependencies of any European power we have not interfered and shall not interfere. But with the Governments who have declared their independence and maintained it, and whose independence we have, on great consideration and just principles, acknowledged, we could not view any interposition for the purpose of oppressing them, or controlling in any other manner their destiny, by any European power in any other light than as the manifestation of an unfriendly disposition toward the United States.[3]*

Simply stated, the U.S. policy was this: Europe was not to establish new colonies in the hemisphere or attempt to regain control of its lost ones. To this, Monroe added a sweetener: The United States in turn would not interfere with the actions of the European powers in their own continent—it would not, in other words, support revolutionary movements overseas.

Monroe had reached this position gradually, after considering a number of options. One was a joint resolution with Britain, whose interests were also threatened by the New World ambitions of the Alliance. But the position favored by the British would have blocked U.S. territorial growth as well as European, something that was vehemently opposed by John Quincy Adams and others who were unwilling to rule out U.S. expansion into California, Mexico, and Cuba. In any case, Adams argued, there was no need for the United States to tie its hands in an agreement with Britain because, even without a formal pledge, Britain's own trade interests would bring it to the defense of any Latin American country that was threatened.

The United States therefore decided to go it alone with a statement that was quite narrow in scope. It specifically ruled out any extension of European colonization or control in the Western Hemisphere, but it said nothing about what role the United States might play in the future of Latin America or the western territories. The Monroe Doctrine was not a law—it was simply a statement of policy and, as such, not binding. Nor was it a treaty—Latin American governments were not consulted. In the United States itself, reaction to the policy was largely favorable. Although some people criticized the doctrine as rash and likely to provoke Europe, most liked the ring of defiance in Monroe's words; commercial interests, not surprisingly, were especially pleased.

The Latin American reaction, however, was mixed. Brazil and Colombia saw the policy as the seed of a hemispheric alliance against Europe and therefore welcomed it. But on the whole, Latin American leaders recognized that their main sources of protection against European ambitions were the width of the Atlantic Ocean and the British fleet.

They also recognized that the Monroe Doctrine was motivated chiefly by self-interest—the United States' desire to protect its trade and territory—and less by a desire to become the standard-bearer of democracy. The Latin American leaders were also wary of U.S. ambitions in the hemisphere. These concerns were reflected when, in 1825, Simón Bolívar called a Pan-American conference to foster unity against Spain—and excluded the United States. (Eventually the United States managed to get on the guest list, but the prospect of Pan-American unity provoked four months of bickering in Congress, led by opponents of foreign "entrapments." Thus, the U.S. delegates were delayed and arrived at the conference site in Panama after the meeting had ended.)

With the exception of Britain, which was content to let the United States share some of the burden of defending Latin America, Europeans greeted the Monroe Doctrine with a mixture of annoyance and derision. Typical was a comment in the Paris newspaper *L'Etoile*: "Mr. Monroe, who is not a sovereign, has assumed in his message the tone of a powerful monarch whose armies and fleets are ready to march at the first signal. . . . [The United States] is bounded on the south by the possessions of the King of Spain, and on the north by those of the King of England. Its independence was recognized only forty years ago; by what right then would the two Americas today be under its immediate sway from Hudson's Bay to Cape Horn?"[4]

Europeans generally seemed to recognize that Monroe's statement had more bark than bite. In fact, having made the pronouncement, the United States proceeded to largely ignore it for two decades. Into the 1840s, still weak and unwilling to pick a fight with Europe, the United States stood by while the French extracted payments from newly independent Haiti, occupied Veracruz, Mexico, and seized Martín García Island in the La Plata River; and while Britain set up Uruguay as a buffer state between Argentina and Brazil and established footholds in the Falkland Islands and Central America.

Texas and Mexico ›

If the United States ignored European moves in South and Central America, one reason was that its attention was focused nearer to home, on Texas and Mexico. The territorial expansion of the United States was continuing.

Shortly after taking office as president in 1825, John Quincy Adams attempted to purchase Texas from Mexico. He tried again in 1827 without success. President Andrew Jackson, who followed Adams in office, renewed the effort in 1829. Mexicans largely viewed these offers as insults—Texas was a rich and fertile region, and they intended to keep it. But Texas was also far from the center of Mexico and thus remained largely undeveloped. Therein lay the seeds of Mexico's undoing—the fertile and empty lands of Texas were a magnet for U.S. settlers.

Beginning in 1821, settlers from the United States had been allowed to move into Texas and had been granted huge tracts of land. By 1835, there were some thirty thousand Americans in the region, and friction had begun to develop between them and the Mexican authorities. The settlers were supposed to become Mexican citizens and adopt Roman Catholicism, Mexico's official religion. Most, however, were Protestants who continued to see themselves as U.S. citizens. Moreover, the Texans came largely from the southern United States, and they believed that their best chance of achieving wealth lay in reproducing the plantation system of the South and growing cotton. That required slavery, a practice that Mexico frowned on. Mexican attempts to assert firmer control over the region and to impose tariffs on goods imported from the United States were additional thorns in the settlers' sides.

In 1835, the Texans revolted against Mexico and declared their independence as the Lone Star Republic. Although their numbers were small and their army disorganized, they included some tough fighters—men like Sam Houston and James Bowie, and others who had been little short of outlaws in the United States and thus had felt more comfortable operating outside its boundaries. People in the United States immediately rallied to the Texas cause, seeing once again an echo of their own revolution. Their support was made stronger by the fact that they felt kinship with the Texans—these were, after all, people from the United States. For its part, Texas offered land grants to anyone who would volunteer to fight on its side. Hundreds did. The U.S. government was officially neutral. But, with both public opinion and territorial interests favoring the Texans, the government closed its eyes to the volunteer efforts and even sent a detachment of troops across the border into Texas, ostensibly to control Indians there.

The Mexican general Antonio López de Santa

Anna moved quickly to crush the revolt. At the famous seige of the Alamo, two hundred Texans held off an army of five thousand Mexicans for twelve days in the early spring of 1836. All were killed when the Mexicans overwhelmed the fort on March 6. A few weeks later, a Texan force of four hundred men (including many volunteers from the United States) surrendered to the Mexicans at Goliad, and three-fourths of them were slaughtered outright.

Whether outrage over the killings at the Alamo and Goliad fueled the Texans, or whether the Mexicans simply became overconfident with the ease of their victories, the tide then turned. On April 26, 1836, the Texans overwhelmed the vastly larger Mexican army at the battle of San Jacinto. Santa Anna, who disguised himself as a foot soldier and attempted to flee, was captured and forced to sign treaties recognizing Texas, which was to extend as far south as the Rio Grande.

The independence of the Lone Star Republic had been achieved. But Mexico promptly repudiated the treaties, and with such a powerful and hostile neighbor to the south, Texas did not appear to have much future as an independent state. Annexation by the United States seemed the most logical course. But here the Texans met with resistance. The United States had become embroiled in the debate over slavery that would culminate in the Civil War. Northerners opposed admitting Texas to the Union because it might tip the balance in favor of the Southern slave states. Thus, President Jackson stalled, delaying the recognition of the Lone Star Republic until the end of his administration in early 1837.

Once recognized, Texas formally applied for annexation. But Jackson's successor, Martin Van Buren, was not eager to fan the flames of conflict between the North and South. The question of annexation was allowed to simply hang in the air until the fall of 1838. Then the Texans, tired of waiting, withdrew their offer. For the next six years, they played a delicate game of geopolitics to attain their goal. Texas began to forge ties with Britain and, to a lesser degree, France; and the Texans let it be known that they were on the point of accepting British and French guarantees of their independence. The Europeans were as delighted with this prospect as the United States was alarmed by it: It would block U.S. expansion. Finally, in January 1845, the United States annexed Texas, largely to avert this threat.

Mexico promptly protested and broke off diplomatic relations with the United States. The Mexicans had been content to let a weak and independent Texas exist on their borders, but they were angered by what they saw as U.S. incursion in their territory. Other issues were at stake, too—the future of California, which seemed likely to go the way of Texas, and the Texas boundary, which had never been agreed on by the two countries.

It was the issue of the Texas border that brought the two countries to war in 1846, and it was the United States that pressed the issue. The United States claimed territory south to the Rio Grande; Mexico recognized a border farther north, at the Nueces River. President James Polk ordered a force of U.S. soldiers south to the mouth of the Rio Grande, where they built a fort and blockaded the river. When reports reached Washington that

Mexican troops had crossed the river and skirmished with the U.S. force, Polk, claiming that the Mexicans had "shed American blood on American soil," asked Congress to declare war.

In the slightly less than two years of fighting that followed, Mexico lost not only its title to Texas north of the Rio Grande but California and much of New Mexico as well. A few years later, the United States picked up the rest of New Mexico and Arizona in the Gadsden Purchase.

A U.S. Sphere of Influence ›

A substantial number of Americans thought the United States should press south and take all of Mexico. Polk thought otherwise. The country was tired of war, and now that the United States stretched from coast to coast, the urge for territorial expansion lessened. But like presidents before and after him, he recognized that the United States had extensive interests in Latin America. In 1848, when rumors began to circulate that Britain intended to buy the Yucután Peninsula from Mexico, he looked for a way to block the move. He found it in the Monroe Doctrine, reviving that policy and extending it in a new way.

While the original doctrine had barred new European colonization in the region, Polk, in a message to Congress, stated that the United States opposed any transfer of territory to an outside power, even if the inhabitants of that territory approved of the change. The difference was significant. For the first time, without consulting the Latin Americans, the United States claimed a right to control foreign affairs throughout the hemisphere.

Polk also barred the Europeans from interfering diplomatically in Latin America. The Polk Corollary, as the statement became known, would become critical to future U.S. actions in Latin America. Its intent went beyond national security; it was meant to establish a sphere of influence in the Western Hemisphere, permitting the United States to enjoy economic and political advantages in the region without actually occupying territory.

Not surprisingly, the European powers were not quick to acknowledge U.S. dominance in Latin America. During the 1860s, while the United States was rent by the Civil War, England, France, and Spain were able to pursue their ambitions in Latin America unchecked. In the Caribbean, Spain reannexed Santo Domingo in 1861 and scoffed at a U.S. protest based on the Monroe Doctrine. And when Mexico suspended payments on its international debts in July of that year, Britain, France, and Spain sent in a joint force. The British and Spanish soon withdrew, but the French emperor Napoleon III set up a puppet state under Ferdinand Maximilian of Austria. Again, the United States protested, but while the Civil War was in progress, it was in no position to fight the French.

Both the Dominican and Mexican ventures came to an end soon after the close of the Civil War. One reason was that the United States emerged from the war with an army of more than 900,000 men ready to lend teeth to its protests. But there were other factors. In 1865, yellow fever broke out on Santo Domingo, and the Dominicans revolted against Spanish oppression. Spain voluntarily withdrew. The French faced an ongoing revolt in Mexico, led by Benito Juárez. Moreover,

"This Is the House that Polk Built." Taken from
Yankee Doodle, *a humorous weekly published
in New York in 1846. The paper opposed the
Mexican War and made fun of President James Polk.*

maintaining the Mexican puppet was costly, and the effort lacked public support in France. A sizable U.S. army, dispatched to the Mexican border, helped the French ruler make up his mind. In 1866, Napoleon III announced that he would pull out his forces. Maximilian was shot by a Mexican firing squad the next year.

With the Civil War behind it and the major threats to its security removed, the United States set itself on a course of reconstruction and industrial development. And as the country grew stronger, the spirit of expansionism reemerged as well.

FOUR GUNBOATS AND DOLLARS

The late nineteenth century was the era of Manifest Destiny—the belief that North Americans were culturally and racially superior and thus fated to control the affairs of the hemisphere. Even the new theory of evolution put forth by Charles Darwin was pressed into service to support this view. The 1885 book *Our Country*, by the Rev. Josiah Strong, summed up the sentiment: "Having developed peculiarly aggressive traits calculated to impress its institutions upon mankind, [the United States] will spread itself over the earth. If I read not amiss, this powerful race will move down Central and South America . . . and beyond. And can anyone doubt that the result of this competition will be the 'survival of the fittest'?"[1] In other words, Yankee gumption and knowhow would rule the hemisphere, if not the world.

In terms of U.S.–Latin American policy, this view resulted in two thrusts. Throughout the hemisphere, the United States sought to become the dominant factor in trade and economic matters. In the areas closest to its borders, and particularly in the Caribbean and Central America, it sought more extensive control. These efforts reached a peak in the early 1900s under two presidents—Theodore Roosevelt (1901 to 1909) and William Howard Taft (1909 to 1913)—who vastly expanded the reach of the Monroe Doctrine to justify U.S. actions.

Blaine and Pan-Americanism ›

The architect of the U.S. effort to expand its economic role in Latin America during the 1880s was James G. Blaine, who served as secretary of state in 1881 under President James Garfield and again from 1889 to 1893 under William Henry Harrison. A leading figure in the Republican party, Blaine was attuned to the needs of business. As the country became more and more industrialized, one of those needs was for overseas markets for manufactured goods. Latin America, which had been slow to develop its own industry, seemed ideal.

Blaine noted that the U.S. need for raw materials already accounted for a large share of Latin American exports. But Latin America preferred to import its manufactured goods from Europe. In the arrangement Blaine envisioned, this would change—the United States and Latin America would become trading partners, with the United States acting in a sort of "big sister" role and providing manufactured goods to the less developed countries to the south. The means to this end would be a customs union, in which trade barriers within the western hemisphere would be eliminated while trade with Europe was restricted.

To win Latin American support for his idea, Blaine called the First International American Conference (or Pan-American Conference), which was held in Washington in 1889–90. Others, including Bolívar, had attempted to hold hemisphere-wide meetings, but this was the first to be well attended. In all, seventeen Latin American countries sent delegates. They were treated to a lightning tour of industrial sites in more than forty U.S. cities and to flowery speeches extolling the proposed customs union. Blaine also proposed that some sort of organization be set up to arbitrate disputes between the countries. To him, this was part and parcel of economic policy: Wars and disputes between Latin American states disrupted trade.

For their part, however, the Latin American countries distrusted U.S. motives. They were not adverse to the ideas of lowering trade barriers and developing closer commercial ties with the United States—for the most part, they subscribed to the principles of free trade—but they preferred individual trade agreements to the idea of a customs union. And they were concerned about what they saw as continued U.S. expansionism. They had reason to mistrust Blaine. In his first brief tenure as secretary of state, he had made a bid to set up U.S. fortifications in Panama.

Blaine had also attempted to act as a broker in disputes between Mexico and Guatemala, Costa Rica and Colombia, and Chile, Peru, and Bolivia. To Latin Americans, his somewhat ham-handed attempts at arbitration amounted to blatant interference. Costa Rica and Colombia had even opted to ask Europeans to arbitrate their dispute instead. In Peru, Blaine had been accused of acting out of personal interest—it was charged that he had a stake in a plan to develop that country's rich guano and nitrate beds. Thus, his proposals for the customs union and international arbitration were politely but coolly received. The conference did have one tangible outcome: the founding of the Pan-American Union, an organization designed to promote understanding and the flow of information between the countries of the hemisphere.

Lack of other formal agreements, however, did not prevent the United States from pressing for dominance in Latin America, particularly in the Caribbean and Central America, regions that the country saw as increasingly vital to both its security and its economic well-being.

Cuba ›

Since colonial times, the Caribbean islands had been a major factor in North America's trade. But as the United States grew stronger, these islands took on new importance. Several of the major islands—Cuba, Hispaniola (shared by Haiti and, after 1865, the Dominican Republic), Puerto Rico—were so close offshore as to be viewed by the proponents of Manifest Destiny as inevitable targets for absorption. And, perhaps more important, these islands guarded the ocean passage to the Gulf of Mexico and the east coast of Central America. Even before firm plans for an east-west canal had been made, people in the United States realized that whoever controlled the Caribbean would also control access to this route.

Cuba—the closest, largest, and (with its extensive sugar plantations) perhaps richest of the islands—was seen as especially important. Right after the Mexican war, sentiment for annexation had been high—"We have New Mexico and California! We will have Old Mexico and Cuba!" predicted an 1848 editorial in *De Bow's Commercial Review*.[2] Up to the Civil War, there had been another reason for annexing Cuba: slavery. Supporters of slavery were seeking to increase their territory (and thus their representation in government), and the institution already existed in Spanish Cuba.

The United States had first tried to buy Cuba from Spain, offering as much as $100 million in 1848. When the offer was turned down, the United States had officially dropped the matter. But private citizens had not. A Venezuelan adventurer, General Narciso López, offered a plan. He would invade Cuba, the population would rise up and declare independence, and then the United States would annex the island. Many Americans enlisted under his banner or offered financial support, and from 1849 to 1851 López organized three expeditions. The first was blocked by U.S. authorities; the second fled Cuba when the Cubans failed to rise up as predicted; and the third ended in tragedy—the Spanish soundly defeated the invaders, shot López and fifty of his followers, and condemned a hundred others to penal servitude.

The incident had led to bitterness between Spain and the United States, but it hadn't dampened American enthusiasm for Cuba. The United States had attempted again to buy the island in 1854, and, secretly, several government officials had begun to make plans to take Cuba by force if Spain refused to sell. But word of the plan leaked out, prompting a chorus of opposition from Europeans and antislavery forces in the United States, and it was dropped.

The Cuban issue had reemerged after the Civil War, when Cubans revolted against Spanish rule in 1868. Popular support for the rebels had been high in the United States. But the government, occupied with the problems of reconstruction, had resisted pressures to get involved. During the same time, U.S. Secretary of State William H. Seward—one of the leading expansionists of the day—had negotiated both with Denmark to buy the Virgin Islands as well as with the tottering, debt-ridden government of the Dominican Republic for virtual annexation. But both plans had met with opposition in Congress. Beset by revolutions, debts, and natural disasters that ranged from earthquakes to hurricanes, the Caribbean was seen as more trouble than it was worth.

By the end of the century, however, U.S. attitudes had changed. Expansionist sentiment was at a peak. When Cubans revolted again in 1895, the United States was ready and willing to take action.

Much of the U.S. motivation was economic—Americans by this time had some $50 million invested in Cuba, and their holdings were literally being torn apart by the fighting between the Spanish and the rebels. Popular feeling against Spain was also stirred up by the press. Two leading newspapers of the day, Joseph Pulitzer's New York *World* and William Randolph Hearst's New York *Journal*, reached the peak of yellow journalism as they battled for circulation with screaming headlines and exaggerated stories of Spanish atrocities in Cuba. "Blood on the roadsides, blood in the fields, blood on the doorsteps, blood, blood, blood!" screeched the *World* in May 1896. "Is there no nation wise enough, brave enough, and strong enough to restore peace in this bloodsmitten land?"[3]

Clearly, the *World* had U.S. intervention in mind. And in 1898, with the rebellion continuing, the United States sent the warship *Maine* to Havana. The visit was intended to be friendly but also to remind the Spanish that the United States would protect its interests. But on February 15, the *Maine* struck an underwater mine in Havana harbor and sank, along with all 250 men aboard. Blame for the explosion was never officially fixed, but, with the help of the newspapers, the public laid it firmly at Spain's door. Within a month, the United States had declared war on Spain.

Significantly, the declaration disavowed any intention to annex Cuba. Many people in the United States respected the Cubans' wish to be free; others recognized that if Cuba remained outside the United States, its lucrative sugar trade could be carried on duty-free. Just as significantly, the Cuban revolutionaries did not appeal to the United States for aid. Suddenly, however, they found their revolution taken over by the power to the north.

When the U.S. warship Maine *sank in Havana harbor, the press and the public blamed the Spanish.*

After a U.S. victory in the short and decisive Spanish-American War, Cuba became a U.S. protectorate. Under this arrangement, the United States could establish naval bases on the island and intervene in Cuban affairs at will, and Cuba could not permit another foreign power to gain control of the island. The agreement (incorporated into the new Cuban constitution as the Platt Amendment) also granted the United States reductions in tariffs and other favorable trade terms. The result was that American investments in Cuba quadrupled, and exports to the island increased eightfold, within twenty years.

The Spanish-American War brought other territories to the United States: Puerto Rico and, in the Pacific, Guam and the Philippines. Thus, by the end of the 1800s, the United States had emerged as the dominant power in the Caribbean and as an important world power as well.

The Panama Canal ›

While the United States was achieving dominance in the Caribbean, interest in some type of canal across Central America was growing. With California developing, the two main routes that linked it to the east—overland across the continent and by sea around Cape Horn—were increasingly inadequate. A route across Central America would cut travel time significantly. Even as the war with Mexico was going on, in 1848, Polk had struck a treaty with New Grenada (later Colombia) granting the United States transit rights across the Isthmus of Panama. By 1855, Americans had completed a 48-mile-long railway across the narrow strip of land.

Meanwhile, various plans for a canal had been put forward. Two sites were considered most likely. One would cross the Isthmus of Panama; the other would go through Nicaragua. But a stumbling block to the canal plans lay in Britain's continued interests in Central America. The British had watched the southward expansion of the United States with concern. They were unwilling to give up the lucrative trade they had established with Latin America or to allow the United States to lock up the east-west route across the isthmus. They already had a toehold in Central America, in the colony of British Honduras (now Belize). In 1848, resurrecting an old claim of a British protectorate over the Mosquito Indians on the east coast of present-day Nicaragua, they had siezed Greytown (San Juan) at the mouth of the San Juan River, a city that might serve as the eastern terminus of a canal.

Alarmed, the United States had opened negotiations with the British. The result was the Clayton-Bulwer Treaty of 1850, in which the two sides agreed to cooperate in building and maintaining a canal, with neither attempting to control it. On territorial claims, the treaty was vague. The Clayton-Bulwer Treaty simply stated that neither side would occupy, colonize, or exercise dominion over Central America—words that could be interpreted in various ways. As vague as its wording was, however, the Clayton-Bulwer Treaty marked the first time that a European power had accepted the general principles outlined in the Monroe Doctrine. The British were prepared to grant that the

United States had interests in Central America and to respect those interests.

Even so, the treaty didn't end friction between the powers—the United States continued to chafe at British presence in Central America, and in 1854 a U.S. naval vessel shelled Greytown after an American diplomat was injured in street riots there. Moreover, the treaty was enormously unpopular in the United States because it appeared to close off southward expansion. And when, in the late 1800s, the United States saw a growing need for a canal, the Clayton-Bulwer Treaty stood in the way.

Once again, it was a threat from Europe that brought matters to a head. In 1879, a French company headed by Ferdinand de Lesseps, builder of the Suez Canal, began to develop plans for a canal at Panama. De Lesseps actually began construction in 1881, but his workers soon ran into difficulties digging through the hard rock of the Continental Divide and battling yellow fever and malaria. By 1889, the company was bankrupt.

A new French firm took over the construction, and the French government was on the point of guaranteeing investment in the venture. Alarmed by the thought that France might control this vital route, U.S. President Rutherford B. Hayes adopted a new policy: Any canal built across the isthmus should be under American control, "virtually a part of the coast line of the United States."[4]

The United States then began negotiations with Britain to revise the now-inconvenient Clayton-Bulwer Treaty so that it would be free to carry out this new policy. Britain at first would have none of it. But British influence in Latin America was declining, and the British were occupied with concerns elsewhere in their empire. By the end of the century, they were ready to grant that the United States was the dominant power in Central America. The result was the Hay-Pauncefote Treaty of 1901, which essentially gave the United States a free hand.

Keeping European powers away was only one step in gaining control of a canal, however. The United States also had to ensure that Latin American states would not interfere. Having chosen and obtained rights to the French company's plan for a Panama canal over a competing plan for the Nicaraguan route, the United States began to negotiate with Colombia, which then controlled the isthmus. The result was an agreement that was highly favorable to the United States, granting rights to a six-mile-wide canal zone in exchange for $10 million and annual payments of $250,000. But Colombians were outraged when they heard the terms of the treaty—the isthmus was one of their country's most valuable assets. Some thought the payments were far too low; others thought that the canal zone should not be given up at all. Thus the Colombian Senate rejected the treaty in August 1903.

Theodore Roosevelt, who had become president two years earlier and was one of the main proponents of the canal, denounced the Colombians as bandits and blackmailers who stood in the path of civilization. There was talk that the United States might seize control of the isthmus outright or, failing that, choose the Nicaraguan route for its canal. But soon another option presented itself: a revolt in Panama. Panamanians had long chafed under the rule of Colombian dictators, and they had rebelled a number of times. Now they saw the potential economic benefits of a canal evaporating before their eyes, and they revolted again on November 3, 1903.

The degree to which the United States was involved in this revolution is debated, but it is clear that the U.S. government was fully aware of the rebels' plans. Citing the old treaty that gave it transit rights across the isthmus, it sent a warship to prevent Colombian troops from landing and putting down the revolt. Within fifteen days of the uprising, the United States had recognized the new republic of Panama and struck an agreement on the canal zone. The terms of payment were the same, but the United States gained control of a wider, ten-mile zone within which it would have even more sweeping rights than had been granted in the earlier agreement with Colombia. (The negotiator who represented Panama in these talks was a Frenchman who, once the matter was settled, never returned to Panama—a point that would later add to friction over the agreements.) Work on the canal, which would open in 1914, could begin.

Relations with Colombia, of course, were severely damaged. (The matter was only partly smoothed over by a payment to Colombia of $25 million in 1921.) Other Latin American governments didn't universally spring to Colombia's defense. Many saw advantages to the construction of the Panama Canal. But among Latin American intellectuals, distrust and criticism of the United States grew—the more so since the U.S. action in Panama was only one of a series of moves the country made at this time to protect what it saw as its economic and political interests.

While labor-saving machinery helped greatly in the building of the Panama Canal, manual labor was in great demand. As seen in this 1909 photo, workers were imported from northern Spain to work on the canal.

By the turn of the century, the United States had achieved its goal of becoming the dominant foreign economic influence in Latin America, particularly in Brazil, Mexico, and the Caribbean Basin. United States companies were heavily invested in Latin American railroads, mines, and plantations, and they were rapidly increasing their investments. As Blaine had foreseen, Latin American markets became increasingly important for U.S. exports.

Latin American countries largely continued to adhere to the principles of free trade and, as a result, the trade relationship that grew up often hindered the development of their own industries. Manufactured products from North America and Europe, which were allowed to enter freely, were often of better quality than those produced by the fledgling Latin American industries, and so these industries found it hard to compete. At the same time, Latin American governments faced mounting expenses. They were eager to advance their countries with the development of railroads and other improvements. Many were plagued with civil wars and kept large standing armies. Thus, they welcomed the inflow of money provided by foreign investors. In many cases, Latin American leaders built up mounting foreign debts.

It was a debt crisis that led Theodore Roosevelt to a remarkable expansion of the Monroe Doctrine in late 1904. After years of civil war and internal government corruption, the Dominican Republic was bankrupt and unable to pay debts it owed to Germany, Britain, and other European powers. These countries had already used military force to collect debts in Venezuela. The United States had looked the other way during that episode but was uneasy with the possibility that European navies might soon spring into action in the Caribbean, a few miles off the U.S. coast.

The solution favored by Roosevelt—who was famous for the remark that in foreign affairs the United States should "speak softly and carry a big stick"—was to jump in ahead of the Europeans. He justified his approach by citing the Monroe Doctrine: "In the Western Hemisphere the adherence of the United States to the Monroe Doctrine may force the United States, however reluctantly, in flagrant cases of . . . wrongdoing or impotence, to the exercise of an international police power."[5] In short, the Roosevelt Corollary (as the policy became known) turned the Monroe Doctrine, originally intended to block European intervention, into a vehicle for U.S. intervention. Under this policy, it was no longer necessary for Europeans to provoke U.S. action. The United States could intervene in Latin American affairs anytime it felt the need.

Diplomatic pressure and a show of force by the Navy induced the Dominican Republic to allow the United States to take over its customs houses, the main source of its revenue, early in 1905. By eliminating much of the corruption that had siphoned off these revenues, the United States was able to put the country on a firmer financial footing and reduce its debts, thus eliminating the need for any European action. Control of the customs houses also put them out of the reach of revolutionaries, helping to quiet the political turmoil.

Of course, the action also advanced U.S. interests in the Caribbean at the expense of Dominican sovereignty—and it was sharply criticized by Roosevelt's opponents in the United States as well as by many Europeans and Latin Americans. Still, most people in the United States supported it, Europeans were glad to see the debt payments resume, and even Latin American governments were remarkably mild in their reactions. American dominance in the Caribbean seemed to be widely accepted as natural and inevitable.

Roosevelt used the big stick more forcefully the following year in Cuba, where a revolution broke out partly in response to the continuing U.S. limits on sovereignty. He reflected the paternalistic attitude that colored U.S. relations throughout Latin America at this time when he wrote of the Cubans in 1906: "All that we wanted from them was that they would behave themselves and be prosperous and happy so that we would not have to interfere. And now, lo and behold, they have started an utterly unjustifiable and pointless revolution and may get things into such a snarl that we have no alternative save to intervene—which will at once convince the suspicious idiots in South America that we do wish to interfere after all, and perhaps have some land-hunger."[6]

United States troops landed in Cuba late in 1906 at the invitation of the Cuban government, and they stayed to restore order until 1909. Despite Roosevelt's assurances to the contrary, the Cuban trouble did in fact revive some talk of annexation in the United States. But the desire for territorial expansion was no longer so strong; economic advantage was the order of the day.

Roosevelt's successor, William Howard Taft, brought this approach to full flower with policies that collectively became known as Dollar Diplomacy. Like Roosevelt, Taft believed that the internal troubles of Latin American states posed a threat to the United States because they invited European intervention. And like Roosevelt, he believed that the Monroe Doctrine gave the United States the right to intervene preventively in Latin American affairs. But Taft's view was that, wherever possible, American advantage should be secured with dollars rather than bullets.

To bolster Central American and Caribbean republics and, in the process, push out European interests, Taft encouraged U.S. banks and firms to invest heavily there, promising that the government would protect their investments. Where bankruptcy threatened, he sought to have the United States act as a sort of receiver—taking over customs houses, for example, as it had in the Dominican Republic. Taft saw the process as beneficial to all. It would bring peace, prosperity, and stability to Latin America. It would allow U.S. firms, through control of key industries and trade, to obtain the most favorable terms and turn a handsome profit. By making the Central American and Caribbean states economically dependent on the United States, it would ensure that they remained in the U.S. sphere of influence. And where dollars didn't suffice to establish U.S. economic dominance, Taft was prepared to use the "big stick" of military intervention. This was the case in Nicaragua.

When Taft took office in 1909, the Panama Canal was just a few years away from completion.

These gates at the upper lock of the
Panama Canal are practically finished.

Central America, which up until then had taken a back seat to the Caribbean in American interests, suddenly loomed larger in importance—and bankruptcy and civil disorders were widespread there. Nicaragua, as the site of the alternate canal route, posed particular problems. It had long been torn by rivalry between two parties, the Liberals and the Conservatives (each represented opposing factions in the landowning elite). In the early 1900s, its ruler was the Liberal José Zelaya, who had seized power in 1893. Zelaya had little use for the United States and was rumored to be considering selling canal rights to Japan or Britain. Having invested heavily in the Panama Canal and expecting to benefit fully from control of the east-west trade that would pass through it, the United States was in no mood to entertain such ideas.

Encouraged by U.S. business interests, the Conservatives revolted and deposed Zelaya in 1909. The United States then moved to establish economic control. It refused to recognize the new Conservative government until Nicaragua arranged to refinance its foreign debt through American banks. When public feeling in Nicaragua turned out to be strongly against this, the United States waved its big stick and sent a warship into Nicaraguan waters. The loan was approved. Next, an American official was installed as collector-general of customs in Nicaragua.

By 1912, the United States virtually controlled Nicaragua's economy. Events then took a predictable course. When a revolt broke out, the United States moved to protect its interests by sending in some 2,500 marines. United States forces, at varying levels of strength, would maintain a nearly constant presence in Nicaragua for the next two decades. Meanwhile, the United States obtained various concessions from the Nicaraguan government, including the perpetual right to build a canal across the isthmus, leases allowing the U.S. Navy to establish coaling stations on offshore islands, and other rights.

At Taft's urging, American banks also poured capital into the debt-plagued Haitian National Bank and secured U.S. interests in that country. Elsewhere, however, not all such efforts were successful. Attempts to have U.S. investors refinance the foreign debts of Honduras, for example, ended when the Senate rejected the treaty that would have made the deal possible. But private means could accomplish the goal as well. After 1899, when it began operations in Honduras, the United Fruit Company increased its stake until it controlled not only the country's chief export (bananas) but also its railway (which the company built) and shipping.

The growing U.S. stake in Latin America led to yet another corollary to the Monroe Doctrine. This interpretation, expressed by Massachusetts Senator Henry Cabot Lodge and adopted by the Senate in 1912, barred the transfer of Latin American property from U.S. firms to non-U.S. firms. The immediate cause of Lodge's pronouncement was Magdalena Bay, a body of water in Lower California that had potential as a naval base. The bay was held by a U.S. syndicate, and rumor had it that the group would sell to a Japanese company. Lodge saw a potential risk to U.S. security if the bay were in foreign hands.

The Lodge Corollary was little more than a footnote to the Monroe Doctrine, yet it illustrates the degree to which Monroe's original ban on European colonization was expanded over the years. Of far greater importance to Latin America at this time was the scope and nature of the growing U.S. economic involvement. Because that involvement tended to perpetuate Latin America's dependence on exports of raw materials and agricultural products, it discouraged the development of industry. Moreover, to protect its economic stake, it was in the United States' interest to preserve the status quo in politics and society—the supremacy of the elite, landowning families. This meant that poverty remained the lot of the vast majority of Latin Americans. It was a recipe for trouble.

FIVE   SHIFTING POLICIES

As the U.S. stake in Latin America increased, so did the need to protect American "lives and property" there. Into the 1930s, U.S. troops intervened (sometimes repeatedly) in Cuba, Haiti, the Dominican Republic, Guatemala, Honduras, Nicaragua, Panama, Colombia, and Mexico. The U.S. government tended to brand its opponents in these countries as "bandits." Some probably were. More often, however, the unrest that U.S. troops moved to put down was prompted by nationalism and concern about the impact that the Colossus of the North was having on its neighbors to the south.

But despite these repeated military interventions, new threads began to appear in U.S. policy. The first shift came under President Woodrow Wilson, who succeeded Taft in 1913. Wilson was an outspoken foe of banks and big business, and he denounced the goals of Dollar Diplomacy. In their place, he substituted the ideals of democracy. Yet for Latin Americans, the shift meant little—Wilson intervened in their affairs fully as much as Roosevelt and Taft. And Wilson's actions no less than those of his predecessors led to sour relations with Latin American states. Mexico, which was in turmoil as Wilson took office, illustrates the point.

Mexico and Morality ›

Since 1877, Mexico had been under the iron rule of the dictator Porfirio Díaz. The stability of his government had produced a safe climate for foreign investment, and the country's wealth—particularly its oil fields—made it a magnet. By 1913, the United States had about $1 billion invested in Mexico. But while foreigners and the Mexican elite shared in the bonanza, the vast majority of Mexicans were landless peons who lived in grinding poverty. Revolution was inevitable, and it came in 1910 under the leadership of Francisco Madero. In May 1911, Madero succeeded in driving the aging Díaz into exile.

Madero advocated land reform—breaking up Mexico's vast estates—as a means of redistributing the wealth of the country and improving the lot of the poor. But his dreams of reform were short-lived. Early in 1913, he was deposed and killed by Victoriano Huerta, who opposed land reform and showed all the signs of restoring a Díaz-type dictatorship. The European powers welcomed the change as a return to stability and promptly recognized Huerta's government. United States business interests were equally pleased, and they expected Wilson to do the same. But the new president was troubled by the way Huerta had usurped power and choked off a democratic movement, and he abhorred the murder of Madero. Thus, he refused to recognize or deal with Huerta's government. In a speech at Mobile, Alabama, in October 1913, he gave his rationale: "We dare not turn from the principle that morality and not expediency is the thing that must guide us and that we will never condone inequity because it is most convenient to do so."[1]

Officially, Wilson's policy was neither to recognize Huerta's government nor to intervene in Mexican affairs. In practice, however, the U.S. cold shoulder put pressure on Huerta. Huerta's government was soon faced with revolt—Francisco Villa, Venustiano Carranza, and others took up the revolutionary cause—and the situation in Mexico rapidly degenerated toward anarchy. American investors were furious. Not only were they losing profits, but a number of Americans were killed in the Mexican fighting. They demanded that Wilson send in troops to restore order. He not only resisted their pressure but lifted an arms embargo that had been imposed against Mexico, allowing weapons to reach the revolutionary fighters.

The situation came to a head in April 1914, when a U.S. Navy whaleboat called at the Mexican port of Tampico to take on supplies. A group of Mexican soldiers mistakenly arrested the whaleboat crew for violating martial law. Although the sailors were released almost immediately, along with an oral apology, the commander of the U.S. Navy demanded a more formal apology and a 21-gun salute to the American flag. The Mexicans balked. This trivial incident provided Wilson with an excuse to intervene against Huerta. Saying that the honor of the country was at stake and that the Tampico incident was the latest in a long string of abuses, he won permission from Congress to send in troops.

On April 21, the United States seized the port of Vera Cruz, thus blocking a large arms shipment destined for Huerta's army. The United States and Mexico seemed headed for war. However, at the last minute, mediators from Argentina, Brazil, and Chile were able to work out a face-saving compromise that averted a full-scale fight. But for Huerta, the game was up—with the revolutionaries gaining in strength and the United States prepared to take up arms against him, he fled the country in July.

Huerta was succeeded by Carranza, and the United States recognized Carranza's government in 1915. Mexico's troubles—and the U.S. role in its affairs—were far from over, however. Carranza proved slow to institute the reforms that were the banner of the revolution, and Pancho Villa soon revolted against him. A rough-hewn and popular leader, Villa was a vehement opponent of foreign investment. In January 1916, a group of his followers killed eighteen U.S. mining engineers in Santa Ysabel, in northern Mexico. A few months later, Villa crossed the border and raided the town of Columbus, New Mexico, leaving seventeen Americans dead.

In the outcry over these incidents, some Americans called for nothing less than the complete occupation of Mexico. Wilson, who had renounced territorial expansion, took a more moderate course. With Carranza's permission, he sent in a force of twelve thousand men to capture Villa.

But the U.S. troops failed in that goal and, as the force increased and plunged deeper into Mexico, soon wore out their welcome. After several clashes with Mexican troops and Carranza's repeated demands that the force be withdrawn, Wilson ordered the troops home in February 1917. By this time, the United States faced troubles elsewhere—the country was just weeks away from entering World War I.

Wilson's actions in Mexico have been described as a sort of moral imperialism, as opposed to territorial or economic imperialism. During his time in office, he also sent U.S. Marines into Haiti and Santo Domingo, in both cases to restore order. (He also purchased the Virgin Islands from Denmark in a move to block possible German control of those islands.) A firm believer in democratic ideals, he sought to implant them in Latin America with almost missionary zeal. This new turn in policy was largely unfruitful, however. In the Caribbean, it produced only a continuation of the status quo. In Mexico, it promoted turmoil and fanned growing resentment of the United States. A new Mexican constitution introduced by Carranza in 1917 not only called for land reform but also established a new principle: that Mexico's oil and mineral wealth belonged to the country, not to foreign investors. Although U.S. firms held on to their investments for the time being, the issue would resurface later.

Away from Intervention ›

The conflict of World War I had little direct effect on Latin America. Mexico, Argentina, Chile, and several other states remained neutral. Brazil and the U.S.–dominated countries of Central America and the Caribbean either broke off relations or declared war with Germany in support of the United States, but they were not touched by the fighting. Indirectly, however, World War I had important economic effects. Trade with Europe was disrupted at the same time that the United States' demand for raw materials increased in step with its war effort. Thus, the Latin American economies became even more dependent on U.S. markets.

The years immediately after the war saw the seeds of a second new thread in U.S.–Latin American policy: a trend toward less intervention. Wilson's actions in Mexico and in the Caribbean had been unpopular at home as well as in Latin America and were an issue in the presidential campaign of 1920. Presidents Warren G. Harding and Calvin Coolidge, who followed him, took a less moralistic tone and attempted to steer a quieter course in their dealings with countries to the south. The marines were withdrawn from Santo Domingo in 1924 and from Nicaragua in 1925.

But the shift was still more one of tone than of substance. The United States retained control of Santo Domingo's customs houses. Marines were still stationed in Haiti. And the marines were back in Nicaragua within two years, when the old conflict between Liberals and Conservatives erupted anew. The U.S. forces supervised elections, trained Nicaragua's National Guard, and stayed on until 1933 to fight a holdout rebel force led by Augusto César Sandino. Their withdrawal left a power vacuum that was promptly filled by the National Guard. Its leader, Anastasio Somoza García, seized power and established a stable but repressive dictatorship. Sandino—a bandit to his opponents but a patriot to many Nicaraguans—was murdered in 1934 after he had surrendered his arms.

The U.S. involvement in Nicaragua was a major source of friction with the Latin American countries and particularly with Mexico, which was still seething from the U.S. interventions during the Wilson years. At the Sixth International Conference of American States, which met in Havana, Cuba, early in 1928, the United States narrowly headed off the adoption of a resolution stating that no country had the right to intervene in the affairs of another. But within a few years, the United States itself would come to espouse this view.

The real change in policy began with Herbert Hoover, who was elected in 1928. Even before he took office, Hoover set out on a seven-week goodwill tour of Latin America. How much goodwill was generated is debatable, but the trip demonstrated the president-elect's concern over the deteriorating relations with the region. He demonstrated that concern again in his inaugural address, with the statement that "we have no desire for territorial expansion, for economic or other domination of other peoples." Perhaps most important, however, was Hoover's approval of a new interpretation of the Monroe Doctrine. The interpretation, which was set out in a memorandum prepared in 1928 by J. Rueben Clark, then undersecretary of state, saw no justification for the repeated U.S. involvement in Caribbean affairs. According to the Clark memorandum, the Monroe Doctrine was directed against European actions only—what took place within Latin American

*President-elect Herbert Hoover, left,
rides through the streets of Santiago
with President Carlos Ibanez during a
goodwill tour of Latin America.*

countries was the affair of those countries, not the United States.

The Great Depression of the 1930s had the effect of furthering this new policy. As U.S. investors took a beating at home and abroad, they were less eager to pour dollars into the countries south of the border. Thus, there was less reason for the U.S. government to tinker with Latin American affairs. Most of Latin America, meanwhile, suffered greatly in the Depression. With economies that were tied to the export of raw materials, chiefly to the United States, Latin American incomes shriveled as foreign industrial production slowed. The U.S. Smoot-Hawley Tariff Act, which imposed high fees on imports, compounded their troubles.

The result was deepening poverty and, along with it, political unrest. For once, however, the United States stayed out of the picture during most of the troubles of the 1930s. When a revolution broke out in Brazil, the United States simply embargoed arms to the rebels and took no further steps to influence the outcome. When the rebels emerged victorious, the United States promptly recognized their government. It was a sharp contrast to Wilson's actions in Mexico a mere two decades earlier.

The new U.S. approach came to full flower under President Franklin Delano Roosevelt, who publicized it as the Good Neighbor Policy. In 1933, Roosevelt took Latin Americans by surprise when, at the Seventh International Conference of American States in Montevideo, Uruguay, the United States supported the same noninterventionist resolution it had opposed at the 1928 conference. The policy was soon tested by events. In Cuba, where the collapse of the world sugar market had produced deep economic problems, a broad popular revolt broke out against the repressive and bloody rule of the dictator Gerardo Machado. The United States went as far as sending warships into Cuban waters, but it held back from direct intervention. With U.S. backing, Fulgencio Batista eventually came to power, and through negotiation won release from the Platt Amendment—the agreement that had given the United States carte blanche for intervention in Cuban affairs—in 1934. That same year, U.S. Marines finally withdrew from Haiti (U.S. financial control ended in 1941).

But the strongest test came in 1938, in Mexico. When Mexican oil field workers went on strike and their foreign employers balked at meeting their demands, the Mexican government decided to enforce the policy that had first been set out in its 1917 constitution: It nationalized the oil industry. The outcry from U.S. oil firms was intense. They demanded that the U.S. government intervene on their side. But Roosevelt resisted the pressure. Instead, he negotiated a compromise under which the oil companies received some $42 million for their holdings. The figure was less than one-sixth of the amount the companies believed that they were owed, but the agreement went a long way toward creating a climate of good relations between the United States and Mexico.

The need for good relations with Latin America was becoming more apparent, too, with the approach of World War II. Both Germany and Italy made attempts to export fascism to Latin America. This was done chiefly through military missions; it was common for Latin American states to

bring in such missions to train their own armies in the latest techniques. Latin Americans also had before them the examples of Spain and Portugal, both of which swung to the right in the 1930s. Thus, extreme right and fascist movements were present in many Latin American countries before the war. As the likelihood of U.S. involvement in the war increased, Roosevelt took steps to see that Latin American states would be on the U.S. side or, at worst, neutral in the conflict, thus ensuring the flow of needed raw materials from the south.

Rather than taking a strong-arm approach, Roosevelt stressed cooperation. He called a special Pan-American conference in 1936, at which he asked for consultation and united (rather than one-sided U.S.) action in the event of a threat from Europe. The mechanism for such consultation was set up by the Declaration of Lima two years later, and during the course of the war the United States and Latin American countries took a number of joint actions. They decreed a "safety belt," or combat-free zone, around Central and South America. They declared that American colonies of European states that had fallen to the fascists (such as the Dutch and French West Indies) could be taken over and jointly administered by American countries. For the first time, the Latin American

U.S. Marines remove luggage from their transports after their twenty-nine-month stay in Haiti ended in August 1934.

countries had been invited to join in a sort of hemisphere-wide Monroe Doctrine.

The United States also negotiated trade agreements that eased the pain of the Smoot-Hawley Tariff Act for Latin Americans. It set up the Inter-American Development Commission to facilitate loans and investment that would help diversify Latin American industry, and it agreed to pay liberal prices for vital resources such as Bolivian tin. The United States also made an all-out effort to counter German propaganda in Latin America, sending out a steady flow of loans, military and economic advisers, cultural programs, and goodwill missions. While Latin American intellectuals sometimes resented being bombarded with Yankee culture, U.S. films, music, and other media gradually emerged as dominant forces in Latin American popular culture. Meanwhile, by offering military supplies and advice at cut rates, the United States was able to displace German military influence in many areas.

The Good Neighbor Policy was by no means selfless—the United States needed Latin America firmly in its sphere of influence as it approached war with Germany. Nor was the policy universally successful. The most difficult situation developed in Argentina, where German influence was strong. Through the 1930s and early 1940s, a series of military and conservative leaders controlled the Argentine government. Meanwhile, the country suffered greatly from the Depression and was particularly resentful of U.S. trade barriers against beef and grain, its main exports. New trade agreements helped ease this friction in 1941, but Argentina refused to join in the various Pan-American resolutions against fascism. A new military regime took power in a coup in 1943; among its leaders was Juan Domingo Perón. This new regime was strongly pro-German at first, but the United States was able to bring diplomatic and economic pressures to bear. Argentina broke relations with Germany and Japan in 1944, and in 1945, when the war was nearly over, actually declared war on the Axis powers.

Meanwhile, Perón, by combining the support of the military and labor groups and outmaneuvering his political rivals, gradually emerged as the most powerful figure in the country. The United States detected a strong tilt toward fascism in Perón and opposed him. But, despite a U.S.–backed campaign that included the release of captured German documents linking the Argentine leader to the Nazis, he was elected president in 1946. The U.S. pressure may actually have worked in Perón's favor in the vote—many Argentinians saw it as unwelcome Yankee meddling.

In the prewar and war years, however, the difficulties with Argentina (and to a lesser degree Chile) were exceptions to the rule. Taken together, Roosevelt's efforts to woo rather than intimidate Latin America were highly successful. The resentment and hostility that had festered in the early years of the century gave way to a climate of cooperation. The United States obtained not only the war materials it needed but also the use of bases in Brazil and elsewhere. With the end of World War II, U.S. influence south of the border was at a peak, not only politically and culturally, but economically as well. The war effort had ended the Depression, and in 1945 the United States was

*Newly elected Argentine President Juan Perón,
left, receives the sash of office
from retiring president Edelmiro Farrell.*

producing half the world's manufactured goods. That in turn increased its need for Latin America's raw materials. Europe, meanwhile, was decimated by the war; most British and French investments in Latin America were sold off to help pay enormous war costs.

With some justification, Latin Americans looked forward to good times after the war. The increased wealth and power of the United States, as well as its increased interest in and cooperative attitude toward their region, boded well for economic development. But right after the war, Latin America found itself put on the shelf as far as the United States was concerned. The U.S. government saw a much greater need to rebuild Europe and Japan than to aid Latin American economies, so U.S. dollars poured east and west rather than south. U.S. interest in Latin America would shortly revive, but with yet another twist.

Just as the United States emerged from World War II with increased power and influence worldwide, so did the Soviet Union. The totalitarian rule and centralized economic system established by the Soviet leader Joseph Stalin were diametrically opposed to the democracy and capitalism espoused by the United States, as were most of the basic beliefs of Communism itself. The Soviet Union, with its stated goal of exporting Communism around the world, was seen as a major threat to U.S. influence abroad and security at home. That threat seemed justified in light of a number of Soviet moves, such as the sealing off of Berlin, just after the war. The two countries thus quickly became embroiled in the Cold War—a worldwide conflict of ideology rather than of arms. This conflict would have a profound impact on U.S. relations with Latin America.

In the late 1940s, the administration of President Harry S. Truman believed that one of the most fertile grounds for Communist expansion lay at its own back door, in Latin America. The continuing poverty of most Latin Americans and the tradition of revolution against repressive regimes appeared to present openings for Marxist ideology. Indeed, Communist parties had already begun to develop, and by 1945 they were represented in the governments of a dozen Latin American countries. In Chile, three members of the cabinet were Communists; and in Brazil, traditionally one of the United States' strongest supporters in the region, the Communist Party won 10 percent of the vote in the 1946 presidential election.

Thus, U.S. attention focused once again on Latin America. The tendency in the United States was to see the threat of Communism in Latin America as one that was imposed from overseas, much as European colonial ambitions had posed a threat in earlier days and as Germany's export of facism had posed a threat before and during World War II. Truman moved to counter the Soviet threat in much the same way that Roosevelt had moved against facism.

The Fight against Communism ›

Politically, Truman pressured Latin American countries to ban local Communist parties and to break off diplomatic relations with the Soviet Union (all but Mexico, Argentina, and Uruguay did so). In an effort to present a united front against the Soviets, Truman forged a military alliance, the 1947 Rio Pact, that stated that an attack on any country in the region would be considered an attack on all. The pact was followed in 1948 by the founding of the Organization of American States (OAS), a regional association that backed the principles of democracy, unity, human rights, and economic cooperation. (The Latin American countries insisted on another principle as well: nonintervention.) In its early years, the OAS often functioned as a rubber stamp for U.S. policies. During the Korean War, for example, the United States successfully urged the OAS to brand the conflict an attack on the United States, thus obtaining Latin American support for the war effort.

Truman also renewed the effort to supply and train Latin American armies and security forces, thus tying them to the United States. Through the 1950s, a number of Latin American countries—including Brazil, Chile, Colombia, Cuba, Nicaragua, Peru, and others—signed agreements under which they received military assistance in exchange for promises to beef up their defenses, reduce trade with the Soviets, and provide the United States with strategic materials.

However, it soon became apparent that the situation was more complex than a simple threat from abroad. While the specifics varied from country to country within Latin America, the Communists were part of three emerging groups in regional politics. Along with other radical reformers, they supported the redistribution of wealth and political power through land reform, the nationalization of industry, and similar tactics. Opposing them were conservatives, mainly the traditional wealthy elite and factions of the military, who wanted to maintain the status quo. Between the two extremes were moderate reformers who rejected the extreme of Communism but were aware that maintaining the status quo would promote both poverty and political unrest. Having learned in the Depression the dangers of relying on exports of raw materials, they saw a way out through industrial development, which they believed would broaden the middle class and improve life throughout society.

Seen in this context, Communism was not simply a threat presented from outside the hemisphere by Soviet ambitions but a symptom of deep social and political ills that were present in the region. The ideology was attractive to many Latin Americans because it promised a quick and radical solution to those problems. The Truman administration showed awareness of this when it began a program of economic and technical aid to Latin America. The program was similar to the Marshall Plan, which had been designed to rebuild industry in Europe, but on a smaller scale. This aid, the Truman administration hoped, would counter the appeal of Communism by promoting the middle course of reform through development.

But the development of industry proved more difficult in Latin America than in Europe—the region lacked a large pool of skilled labor, and in many areas the communication and transportation links needed for industrial development weren't in place. In any case, the effort petered out after President Dwight D. Eisenhower took office in 1953. As a Republican, he favored free market policies and wanted Latin American countries to keep the door open to foreign investment.

For thirty years after World War II, opposition to Communism remained the main guiding force behind U.S.–Latin American policy. Successive U.S. administrations used various methods in their attempts to accomplish the goal—economic aid, diplomatic pressure, direct intervention, secret operations. Meanwhile, nationalism grew stronger throughout Latin America. The people of the region wanted control of their own affairs both politically and economically. Often, nationalism was expressed as opposition to and resentment of the United States. And often, that opposition was interpreted by the United States as a leaning toward Communism. As a result, U.S. actions sometimes served to block reforms. Guatemala provides a case in point.

Guatemala ›

In the early 1950s, Guatemalan president Jacobo Arbenz Guzmán instituted a sweeping reform program that included the nationalization of some of the vast holdings of wealthy landowners, including the United Fruit Company. (At the time, United Fruit was the country's largest landholder and had a major stake in its railroads and shipping as well.) Arbenz also demanded that United Fruit pay taxes on its profits (the company was receiving a return of more than 70 percent on its investments), allow workers to unionize, and pay them a minimum wage. Arbenz also moved to restore relations with the countries of the Communist bloc.

The United States government believed that Arbenz was moving toward Communism, and it saw U.S. interests threatened economically and politically. At a 1954 OAS conference in Caracas, Venezuela, the U.S. government won the adoption of a resolution that once again raised the specter of intervention. The resolution stated: "The domination or control of the political institutions of any American state by the international Communist movement, extending to this hemisphere the political system of an extra-Continental power, would constitute a threat to the sovereignty and political independence of the American states, endangering the peace of America, and would call for a meeting of consultation to consider the adoption of appropriate action in accordance with existing treaties."[1]

Except that it called for cooperative action rather than one-sided steps on the part of the United States, the Caracas Resolution echoed the Monroe Doctrine and the broad interpretation it had been given by Theodore Roosevelt. The United States was unable to obtain OAS support for direct intervention against Guatemala, however, and it was unwilling to send in the marines. Instead, in a strategy that would be repeated elsewhere in Latin America, the U.S. Central Intelligence Agency (CIA) organized a group of Guatemalan exiles into an invasion force. The invasion was successful— Arbenz was overthrown, and the new president, Carlos Castillo Armas, promptly returned the confiscated lands and signed a mutual defense agreement with the United States.

Through the exiles, the United States accomplished its goals by proxy and restored the situation that had existed in Guatemala before Arbenz. But in overthrowing Arbenz, the United States left untouched the deep social problems that had prompted his reforms. Guatemala would shortly embark on a course of repression, coups, rebellions, and human rights abuses that would extend to present times. Meanwhile, although the United States could point to the Caracas Resolution as justification for its intervention, the U.S. role in Guatemala deepened the resentment felt by many reform-minded Latin Americans. When U.S. Vice President Richard Nixon toured eight Latin American countries in 1958, he was met by anti–U.S. demonstrations and riots.

Castro's Cuba ›

As the 1950s drew to a close, the biggest U.S. showdown with Communism was taking shape in the Caribbean. In Cuba, the 1930s revolt headed by Fulgencio Batista had failed to bring any real improvement for the vast majority of people. Batista had stepped down as president in 1944 and permitted open elections. But in 1952, after a period of chaotic politics and worsening economic conditions, he once again staged a coup and took power. From then on, he sought to stifle his opposition as he maintained his position through rigged elections.

Denied the hope of free elections, a number of Batista's opponents (who included many students) took up arms. Among them was Fidel Castro, who was jailed in 1953 for leading an attack on the Moncada Barracks, a military base in eastern Cuba. Released in a general amnesty in 1955, Castro moved to Mexico, where he organized a small invasion force. The force landed in Cuba on December 2, 1956, and was all but wiped out by

*General Batista addresses the Cuban army
after taking over the Cuban government.*

Batista's troops. Castro fled into the mountains with just eleven survivors, and the widespread uprising he had expected his invasion to spark did not materialize. But he persevered, and gradually small bands of supporters began to join his forces.

Faced with growing rebellion, Batista reacted with stern repression. This had the effect of helping to swing public opinion in Castro's favor. By mid-1958, Castro's force was strong enough to hold pitched battles with government troops. On January 2, 1959, he took Santiago, and Batista's rule was over.

As Castro's power had grown, other opposition leaders had met with him and extracted various promises, including pledges to restore a democratic constitution and to hold elections. The promises were never kept. After he came to power, Castro staged war crimes trials that resulted in the execution of more than six hundred people. He also sought to spread his revolution, supporting armed revolts in Haiti, the Dominican Republic, Nicaragua, and Panama. Meanwhile, relations with the United States began to sour rapidly.

Castro saw the enormous economic and political influence that the United States had in Cuba as a threat to his country's sovereignty, and he sought to counter it by increasing the Soviet stake in aid and trade. He also began a radical program of social and economic reform that included the seizure of foreign-owned property. In 1960, he na-

Fidel Castro marches to Havana in January 1959.

tionalized U.S. and British oil interests for refusing to refine imported Soviet petroleum. The United States reacted by refusing to sell arms to Cuba and suspending imports of Cuban sugar—the island's main source of income. After Cuba demanded that the U.S. embassy staff be cut to eleven people, the United States broke off diplomatic relations with the new regime in January 1961. Late in that year, Castro openly declared his conversion to Communism.

As the gulf between the two countries widened and Castro's move toward Communism became increasingly apparent, the United States sought to repeat its Guatemalan success by training and supporting an invasion force made up of Cuban exiles. The seeds of the plan were sown in the Eisenhower era, but it was President John F. Kennedy who decided to go ahead with it. The result was the ill-fated Bay of Pigs invasion in April 1961. The U.S. Navy escorted the 1,200 invaders to Cuban waters, but Kennedy canceled approval of air cover that was to have been provided by Cuban-refugee pilots. Both politically and militarily, the invasion was misconceived from the beginning. It fizzled. In three days of fighting, a hundred members of the invading force were killed and the remainder were taken prisoner.

The Bay of Pigs fiasco had a number of effects. One was to strengthen Castro's power at home and his prestige abroad. With clear proof of the United States' hostile intent, he cracked down freely on his remaining opposition. The flip side of that coin was a lessening in U.S. prestige. Never had a U.S. attempt to influence Latin American affairs failed quite so dismally. The United States abandoned open attempts to overthrow Castro (although it was later revealed that the CIA hatched several plots against the Cuban leader's life). Instead, it focused on diplomatic and economic pressure through the OAS, winning the exclusion of Cuba from that organization.

Then came an incident that turned the soured U.S.–Cuban relations into a threat to world peace. The trouble began in the summer of 1962, when the Soviet Union began to ship missiles to Cuba. By October, U.S. reconnaissance planes had confirmed that medium- and intermediate-range Soviet missile stations were being set up within easy striking distance of the United States.

In the face of a clear threat, Kennedy imposed a blockade aimed at cutting off all shipments of military equipment to Cuba, and he demanded that the Soviets withdraw their missiles. If the missiles were not dismantled, he said, the United States would invade Cuba. The Soviets at first denied that the missiles existed. Once reconnaissance photos of the installations were publicized, however, they were faced with the choice of backing down or risking nuclear war. They backed down—a mere two days before a planned U.S. invasion was to begin. The end of the Cuban missile crisis did not mark the end of the chill in U.S.–Cuban relations, but the United States regained some of its lost prestige through the showdown with the Soviets.

Some historians have argued that through the Bay of Pigs invasion and other actions, the United States actually helped push Castro toward Communism, by presenting a hostile face to his regime. Others have argued that Cuba's drift to Communism was inevitable once Castro came to

LAUNCH POSITION

MISSILE-READY TENT

MISSILE ERECTORS

power. Whatever the case, Castro's ties to the Communist world increased over the following years. He also stepped up his program of exporting revolution throughout Latin America. By 1970, Cuban-backed guerrilla movements had sprung up in more than a dozen Latin American countries. ("Che" Guevara, who directed this effort for Castro, was killed in Bolivia in 1967.) After the Venezuelan government discovered a cache of Cuban arms in late 1963, the OAS imposed a program of economic sanctions designed to pressure Cuba into more acceptable behavior. But massive Soviet subsidies kept the Castro regime and its program of revolution alive.

Meanwhile, the failure of the Bay of Pigs invasion and the extreme threat posed by the missile crisis underscored the need for a new approach in U.S.–Latin American policy. Kennedy, who had recognized this need even before the Bay of Pigs, had outlined that approach early in 1961, when he unveiled a new program called the Alliance for Progress.

This reconnaissance photo (top left) taken in October 1962 showed a missile base at San Cristobal, Cuba. The Soviet vessel Volgoles, *with missiles on board, is outbound from Cuba after the missile crisis. A U.S. Navy radar ship is alongside (bottom left).*

The Alliance for Progress ›

The Alliance for Progress was a broad-based aid program aimed at triggering social and economic changes in Latin America. In effect, the United States would thwart Communism by seizing the banner of reform. The program represented acceptance of the view that greater stability and security would come through economic development and a broadening of the middle class, along with greater democracy in government. Once these reforms took root, U.S. policymakers reasoned, Latin Americans would be more likely to see their interests as coinciding with those of the United States.

The program called for some $20 billion in funds from government and private sources to be pumped into Latin America over a ten-year period. Latin American governments would submit development plans to a council of economists and other experts. Then the funds would be targeted to achieving the goals set out in those plans. The program's developers hoped that through development, Latin American incomes would gradually increase while becoming more evenly distributed, lifting more people out of poverty. Along with development aid came a range of social programs, aimed at decreasing illiteracy, infant mortality, and other problems. Peace Corps volunteers were soon making their way to remote Latin American villages.

Because it recognized that the threats of Communism and instability stemmed from Latin America's social and economic problems and that those threats could be reduced by promoting moderate reform rather than retaining the status quo, the Alliance for Progress marked a change in U.S. policy. Because the United States ultimately controlled the purse strings of the aid program, however, the program was criticized for promoting only development that would not damage U.S. interests and investments. And in the area of social reform, the United States tended to underestimate the degree to which conservative forces would struggle to preserve the status quo. Often, moderate reformers were unable to achieve any meaningful change in areas of land reform or the redistribution of wealth: If they moved too quickly toward change, they faced the threat of a military coup.

The Alliance for Progress was announced with a great fanfare of publicity. Less openly, the United States used diplomatic pressure to bring about democratic elections—and sometimes attempted to influence their outcome. In 1964, for example, the United States quietly spent some $3 million on the election campaign of the moderate reformer Eduardo Frei in Chile. The United States also extended support to some less than democratic changes; it enthusiastically welcomed, for example, a military coup that in 1964 overthrew the highly nationalistic (and somewhat ineffective) government of João Goulart in Brazil. The military government that took over focused on economic development but ignored social reform as it increased repression, imprisoning and torturing its opponents.

Even as the aid programs were getting under way, the United States also stepped up military aid in Latin America, particularly in countries that were threatened by leftist guerrilla movements.

With U.S. help, Latin American armies and police forces obtained the tools and training they needed to fight rebels and terrorists—and to suppress their opponents. These less publicized aspects of U.S. policy in the 1960s—with their focus on military strength and political influence—showed that the United States had no intention of abandoning its sphere of influence in Latin America. That point was made clear in 1965, when the United States sent troops into the Dominican Republic.

Growing Resentment ›

Rafael Trujillo, the leader of the Dominican Republic and one of Latin America's most repressive dictators, had been assassinated in 1961. In open voting following his death, Juan Bosch was elected president. Bosch was a popular reformer and initially had the support of the United States. As he began to develop plans for redistributing land and other major reforms, however, U.S. support drained away. Bosch soon faced a powerful conservative opposition, and in 1963 he was deposed in a military coup.

The new Dominican regime soon found itself faced with an armed insurgency; to analysts in the United States, that insurgency had the earmarks of Communism. President Lyndon Johnson, who had vowed to continue the Alliance for Progress, was eager to keep another Castro-like regime from coming to power. His response was to send in more than twenty thousand marines and paratroopers to restore order.

The Johnson administration had several justifications for the action. The U.S. troops were invited by the Dominican regime (although the legitimacy of that regime was open to question) and, within two days of the invasion, the OAS approved the action and the creation of an international peace force. The troops left after Joaquin Balaguer was elected president in 1966. But the invasion, which ended a hiatus of more than thirty years in U.S. armed intervention in Latin America, seemed to contradict the reformist rhetoric of the Alliance for Progress. In short, it fueled considerable resentment throughout Latin America. Once again, the United States was seen as imposing its will by force.

In fact, despite the high goals of the Alliance for Progress and the massive publicity given to that program, resentment of the United States had been growing even before the Dominican action. In the Canal Zone, riots between Americans and angry Panamanians erupted in 1964. The violence led to a short break in relations between the United States and Panama and also made plain the need for a complete renegotiation of the basic treaties giving the United States control over the Canal Zone.

But, although negotiations with Panama were begun, U.S. concern over Latin America lessened in the late 1960s. Attention increasingly focused on the country's growing involvement in Vietnam, and the problems of Latin America seemed less important. President Richard Nixon, who took office in 1968, espoused the goals of social reform and development in the region. But in practice, his administration was more concerned with security. A report prepared by Nelson Rockefeller, who toured Latin America on a presidential mission in 1969 and would later become vice-president, advocated a range of new programs, most of which were not adopted by the administration.

This grafitti in Santo Domingo in the
Dominican Republic clearly shows the
Dominicans' opinion of U.S. intervention.

Development once again was left more to the private sector, in a policy referred to as "mature partnership." The administration did pay heed to one aspect of the Rockefeller report: a proposal to support the military as a force for constructive social change. Military aid to Latin American governments continued unabated.

The Nixon administration was soon faced with a unique problem: the first freely elected Marxist leader in Latin America, Salvador Allende of Chile. Allende won the presidency in 1970, after the more moderate reforms advocated by his predecessor Frei had run aground. The United States had already expended considerable funds and effort quietly attempting to undermine Allende's leftist party. After his election, it stepped up its efforts, secretly funding opposition groups, stimulating anti-Allende news stories, discouraging private investment in Chile, and blocking Chile's access to international loans. The U.S. actions contributed to a decline in Chile's economy and to rapid polarization in its politics. In 1973, Allende was deposed and killed in a coup that had the support of many political moderates as well as conservatives.

While the United States was not solely responsible for the 1973 coup in Chile, its role was widely publicized in the press and in Senate hearings after the fact. Once again, the image was one of high-handed intervention. By now, that image was unpopular at home as well as in Latin America. The U.S. involvement in Vietnam had shown where intervention might ultimately lead, and the public was in no mood to support such actions elsewhere.

The United States remained the single most powerful foreign force in Latin America, but during the 1970s it found its influence declining. The decline was firstly economic. In the years just after World War II, Latin America had received more than half its imports from the United States, and the United States had absorbed more than 45 percent of the region's exports. By the late 1970s, the figures had dropped to about 35 percent; meanwhile, trade with Western Europe and Japan increased.

The shift was most pronounced in South America. United States trade with Central America and the Caribbean remained strong. But the nature of the trade changed, too. While many Latin American countries continued to depend on a few major export products, most were beginning to diversify into new crops and manufactured goods. Industrial growth in turn was bringing changes in society. Since the 1930s, people had been moving to the cities in growing numbers, and in countries where the growth was strongest, the social fabric now included a larger middle class and a new group, the urban poor.

Politically, the picture was also changing. Latin American countries increasingly showed a desire to handle their own affairs, without interference from the United States. To lessen their dependence on U.S. military aid, many began to purchase arms from other sources, including Israel and the European countries. Brazil and several other countries began to manufacture their own weapons. Latin American countries began to take a more active role in regional associations that excluded the United States and in international associations of developing countries. In doing so, they were part of a new voice in international politics—that of the Third World, developing countries that were aligned with neither the United States nor the Soviet Union. More and more, these countries saw the global conflict of the Cold War as harmful to their interests.

By the mid- to late 1970s, several other developments had helped convince many people that the United States needed a new policy in Latin America—one that had broader goals than simply containing Communism. Chief among these developments was the Arab oil embargo of 1973 and subsequent decisions by the Organization of Petroleum Exporting Countries (OPEC) to sharply raise oil prices. While the thrust of these moves came from the Arab countries of the Middle East and had political overtones stemming from problems in that region, the oil price hikes affected U.S.–Latin American relations as well—several

Latin American countries, including Mexico and Venezuela, were major oil producers. The United States was forced to take a fresh look at its policies toward these countries.

Along with the changing situation in Latin America had come a change in the mood of the United States. Vietnam had left Americans gun-shy of foreign military involvement; through the 1970s, the number of U.S. military advisers in Latin America dropped from more than eight hundred to fewer than one hundred. Public opinion had likewise turned against policies that, with the goal of stopping Communism, kept repressive dictators in place. The Watergate scandal, which led to the resignation of President Nixon, left a distaste for undercover operations, so that the revelation of actions such as the undermining of Salvador Allende in Chile produced a public outcry in the United States as well as in Latin America.

Gradually U.S. policies began to reflect these new concerns. The change began late in the Nixon administration, when Secretary of State Henry Kissinger proposed what he called a "new dialogue" with Latin American countries. But, apart from holding discussions with Panama on the future of the Canal Zone and secret talks with Cuba on the possibility of restoring diplomatic relations, the United States under Nixon and his successor, Gerald Ford, did little in concrete terms to improve relations with Latin America. The focus of U.S. policy was elsewhere—on ending the Vietnam conflict, on opening diplomatic relations with China, and on dealing with the Soviet Union. Meanwhile, a number of incidents—an eight-month delay in the appointment of a U.S. ambassador to

Mexico in 1969, new import surcharges imposed without warning in 1971—continued the friction with Latin America.

Carter's New Focus ›

When President Jimmy Carter took office in 1977, it seemed that U.S. policy would shift much more dramatically. Carter was openly critical of the way U.S. actions had been influenced by what he called an inordinate fear of Communism. His foreign policy in Latin America and elsewhere was based on a different view of the world. Rather than seeing international developments in the context of a struggle between East and West—Communism and democratic capitalism—his administration placed more emphasis on North-South issues; that is, the conflicts that often emerged between developed countries (most of which were located in the northern half of the globe) and developing countries (mostly in the southern hemisphere).

In formulating its Latin American policy, the Carter administration drew on the views expressed by a bipartisan group, the Commission on United States–Latin American Relations. Two reports issued by this group, which was chaired by former OAS ambassador Sol M. Linowitz, urged the United States to abandon attempts to dominate Latin American affairs. The group proposed instead several steps to improve relations: new agreements on the Panama Canal, better relations with Cuba, greater support for democracy and human rights, and greater responsiveness to the region's economic concerns.

One of the administration's first steps, then,

was to complete negotiations with Panama over the Canal Zone. Under the agreements that were finally hammered out, control of the Canal would gradually be transferred to Panama by the year 2000. The treaties included provisions for joint defense of the waterway, a guarantee that it would remain open to ships of all nations, and a U.S. agreement to provide Panama with economic and military aid if necessary. The United States also retained the right to intervene if the Canal were closed for any reason. Some Panamanians had reservations about the new agreements, believing that they still gave the United States too large a role in their affairs. But in October 1977, they voted two to one to accept the plan.

The treaties faced more opposition in the U.S. Senate, where they had to win a two-thirds majority to be ratified. Opponents scored the agreements as a giveaway of U.S. property and a blow to national security. They mistrusted the promises of Panamanian leader Omar Torrijos to keep the canal open and neutral, pointing out that he was a dictator with a long record of human rights abuses. Moreover, the Canal was something of a symbol to many Americans, standing for U.S. determination and skill. The administration managed to win ratification in the spring of 1978, after Torrijos promised to end repression even if he had to resign to do so. (Torrijos did resign as head of government in 1978, appointing a civilian president. But as head of the National Guard, he remained the most powerful person in the country until his death in a plane crash in 1981.)

Shortly after Jimmy Carter took office, he also began to take steps to improve relations with Cuba. In April 1977, the first direct talks between U.S.

and Cuban officials since 1961 took place. The talks led to an agreement on fishing rights; and in September, the two countries opened missions in each other's capitals. There was much optimism that they would soon resume formal diplomatic relations. But that optimism quickly faded as Cuba became heavily involved in Angola and several other African countries. Some twenty-six thousand Cuban soldiers and military advisers were thought to be aiding Marxist movements in Africa by late 1977. The United States became increasingly critical of the Cuban role, calling it a threat to peace, and was suspicious of Cuba's goals.

Many of Carter's other Latin American initiatives likewise ran aground. For example, the president promised a major new effort to improve relations with Mexico, which, as the fifth largest U.S. trading partner, already held an important place in U.S. foreign policy. But in practice, the two countries' interests were often in conflict. In the late 1970s, Mexico announced the discovery of new oil reserves vast enough to place the country in a league with Saudi Arabia as an oil producer. Thus Mexico soon found itself courted by the energy-hungry industrial countries. The Mexican government made it clear that it was no client of the United States—its oil would be sold at world market prices, and the United States would get no bargain.

Carter agreed that Mexico's oil was Mexico's to sell as the country saw fit. But friction remained between the two countries. Several issues—energy (particularly the importation of Mexican natural gas), trade, and immigration—were especially thorny. Carter promised to work with Mexico to control the flow of aliens who were crossing into the United States illegally in growing numbers. (Mexico contended that taking the illegal aliens back would produce economic chaos at home and argued that only by easing trade restrictions—so that Mexican industry and agriculture could expand and create new jobs—would the problem be solved.) Yet in his first year in office, Carter sent a proposal on the problem to Congress without consulting Mexico.

The United States also abruptly canceled a contract to purchase Mexican natural gas, despite the fact that Mexico had begun to build a new pipeline to the U.S. border. Although a new contract was later worked out, the cancellation produced a chill in relations. Carter received a cool, although formally correct, reception when he visited Mexico in 1979.

Elsewhere in Latin America, concern over human rights led the administration to distance itself from authoritarian regimes and to deny military aid to those with the most flagrant records of repression and violence. For example, it cut off military aid to Guatemala, where the military government was accused of using torture and "hit squads" to silence its opponents. The United States also began to establish links with opposition groups, even when they were clearly left of center. But this more tolerant policy changed with time—and in no place more dramatically than in Central America.

Nicaragua and El Salvador ›

When the Marines pulled out of Nicaragua in 1933, they left behind a U.S.–trained National Guard under the command of General Anastasio Somoza García. Somoza soon eliminated his last armed opposition with the killing of the rebel leader Augusto Cesár Sandino, and he emerged as president in a 1934 election in which he was the only candidate. Thus began some forty years of what amounted to a hereditary dictatorship, in which Somoza and his heirs and associates amassed huge fortunes while most of the country fell deeper into economic disarray.

A leftist guerrilla movement began to trouble the regime in the 1960s. Small at first, the movement took the name Sandinista National Liberation Front (after Augusto Sandino) and received support from Cuba. As time went on, it grew in strength, and its support broadened. The Somoza regime became increasingly repressive as it fought to crush the rebellion. As it did so, it alienated the country's moderates and its middle class. By the late 1970s, the Sandinistas had wide support throughout the country, and what had begun as a small uprising had grown into a bloody civil war. Thousands of people were killed in the fighting, and entire towns were destroyed. The economy broke down, and with it public services and medical care.

It was clear that the current ruler, Anastasio Somoza Debayle, was losing control. Other countries of the region began to back the Sandinistas in the fight and called for Somoza to step down. The final blow came when the Carter administration, without actually moving to the Sandinista side, denounced Somoza's brutal human rights violations and cut off most military and economic aid to his government. The dictator resigned and fled into exile in July 1979, and a five-member Sandinista junta took control.

The new government included both moderates and Cuban-trained Marxists. While it was clear that its positions would be far to the left of previous Nicaraguan regimes, it promised to permit political debate and opposition. The United States began to provide aid to help the country rebuild its shattered economy. But the honeymoon was short. Nicaragua soon began to align itself more and more with Cuba. The U.S. attitude became increasingly distrustful as suspicions grew that Nicaragua was aiding revolutions elsewhere, chiefly in neighboring El Salvador.

El Salvador, the smallest and most densely populated of the Central American countries, had been under military rule since 1932. The government represented a small group of landowners, called the Fourteen Families, who held most of the country's wealth. In the 1970s, there were attempts to bring reform through democratic elections, but voting fraud kept the military in control. As in Nicaragua, the result of this (and an increasing number of government human rights violations) was to increase support for leftist guerrillas who hoped to overthrow the government.

Late in 1979, a coup brought a new military-civilian junta to power. This group promised a more moderate course and an end to the harsh repression of the previous government, and it went so far as to begin a land reform program. These moves won it the opposition of both left and right—the landowners, of course, did not want their estates to be broken up, while the leftist rebels wanted faster and more radical reforms.

Reforms bogged down as fighting increased. There were reports of brutality on all sides—guerrillas kidnapped and murdered business leaders, while government troops and right-wing squads were charged with widespread civilian killings, including the deaths of three American nuns in 1980. Meanwhile, evidence grew that Cuban arms were being channeled through Nicaragua to the Salvadoran rebels, who mounted a major offensive in January 1981. President Carter, just days from leaving office, was faced with a rapidly deteriorating situation. He made the decision to back the Salvadoran government with military aid despite its poor record on human rights.

Many Latin Americans had welcomed the Carter administration's stance in favor of human rights and political pluralism. Overall, these policies encouraged a trend toward liberalization in many countries. In Brazil, for example, the military government ended what had been a reign of terror, declaring amnesty for its political opponents and beginning a gradual process of democratization that was to lead to the election of a civilian government. While U.S. policy wasn't directly responsible for the change, it helped create an atmosphere in which the trend toward democracy could flourish. Brazil was not alone in the trend, either—democratic governments came to power in Peru in 1980 and in six other Latin American countries in the following years.

The Carter policies were not universally welcomed, however. To some, they smacked of the sort of moralistic interference practiced by Woodrow Wilson in earlier days. They also did not address the concerns of many Latin Americans. Chief among these concerns were questions of economic aid, trade, and the transfer of technology. With their new and growing industries, Latin American countries wanted better access to international markets, favorable trade agreements, and infusions of capital and technological know-how from the developed world. The Carter administration, faced with growing wage and price inflation and the beginning of an economic recession at home, did less in these areas than many Latin Americans had hoped. Aid did not increase significantly, and, like past presidents, Carter was not keen to negotiate trade agreements that would hurt U.S. industries.

To many Latin Americans, then, the United States appeared once again to be promoting its own interests at the expense of theirs, an impression that was strengthened when the Carter administration ran into the harsh realities of civil war in Central America and began to back away from its stands on human rights and political diversity. And to some people in the United States, the Carter policies had disastrous implications for national security.

The Reagan Years Begin ›

The inauguration of Ronald Reagan as president in 1981 brought a complete reversal in U.S. policy. Rejecting the Carter approach categorically, Reagan returned to the views that had guided policy in earlier years: that U.S. economic and political dominance, particularly in Central America and the Caribbean, was essential for national security; that the greatest threat to that dominance came from the growth of Soviet influence, particularly through Cuba; and that the United States could and should reverse the decline in its influence through a combination of economic aid and investment, diplomatic pressure, and, if necessary, force.

In developing its policies, the Reagan administration drew on the views set out in a 1980 report by a group called the Committee of Sante Fe and on the writings of Jeane Kirkpatrick (who would later represent the United States at the United Nations), particularly an article titled "Dictatorships and Double Standards." These reports blamed the Carter policies for the decline in U.S. influence, saying that they had opened the door to Communism by destabilizing friendly governments such as the Somoza regime in Nicaragua. And they held that Communism, as a totalitarian system, was a greater threat than any pro–U.S. dictatorship, no matter how repressive.

The United States began to put these policies into effect close to home, in Central America and in the Caribbean. If anyone doubted the seriousness of the U.S. intent to oppose Communism in this region, those doubts were firmly dispelled in 1983 with the U.S. invasion of the tiny Caribbean island of Grenada.

Under Carter, the United States had raised no opposition when leftists took power in Grenada in a 1979 coup. The United States had become increasingly uneasy, however, as Grenada had begun to increase its ties with Cuba. (Much of the concern focused on an airstrip that Cuba was building on the island; some analysts believed that the strip was intended for military use.) Then, in 1983, a more radical leftist group staged a second

U.S. troops move toward Grand Anse,
Grenada, in an invasion intended to
cut Grenada's increasing ties with Cuba.

coup and took control. The United States responded by sending in about six thousand troops. The invasion was short: The U.S. forces quickly took control of the tiny island and restored order. Most of the troops were then withdrawn; a handful remained while an interim government was set up. Democratic elections were held within a year.

As the first U.S. military action in the Caribbean in nearly twenty years, the Grenada invasion sparked debate at home and abroad. Those who supported the action argued that the U.S. force was invited by the Organization of Eastern Caribbean States (OECS), under the terms of a mutual defense pact. One of its main goals was to ensure the safety of about a thousand U.S. students on the island, who could have been held hostage or otherwise harmed by a radical leftist regime. The Grenadan leaders removed in the invasion had climbed their way to power with no regard for what the majority of Grenadans might want. Indeed, a poll taken after the invasion found that 90 percent of the island's citizens were glad that the U.S. troops had come. And the fears of Cuban involvement appeared to have some foundation. Cuban "construction workers" at the airstrip, for example, turned out to be an armed force.

Critics of the action, which included a number of U.S. allies, also had strong arguments. For one, the OECS defense pact had been intended to cover foreign aggression, not internal coups, so the invasion had no legal grounds. Critics also argued that the Cuban-Soviet threat had been vastly overstated and that the United States had damaged its image by using force—by returning to the "big stick" tactics of Teddy Roosevelt, the United States appeared no better than the Soviet Union, which maintained its sphere of influence in Eastern Europe with the threat of force.

In terms of its goals, however, the Reagan administration viewed the Grenada invasion as a success. It sent a clear message that the United States would take strong action and use force if necessary to protect its interests. But elsewhere in Latin America, the administration found it far more difficult to reassert U.S. influence. When conflict over the Falkland Islands broke out between Argentina and Britain in 1982, the United States was unable to negotiate a settlement. (It lent its moral support to Britain in the brief war that ensued.) On the positive side, the administration took credit for helping bring about change from military to civilian rule in Argentina, Guatemala, Honduras, Ecuador, and Uruguay, and for contributing to a movement toward democracy in Chile. These changes continued the trend to democracy in Latin America that had gotten under way during the Carter years. During the eight years of the Reagan administration, no coups took place in Latin America. But U.S. pressure was unable to bring about a change to democratic government in Haiti after the fall of the dictator Jean-Claude Duvalier in 1986.

By far the biggest problems for the Reagan administration were those in Central America. Here (and, to a lesser extent, in South America) the administration moved to end some of the restrictions on aid that had been imposed in the Carter years and to increase support to pro–U.S. governments, whether they were democratic or not. (Concern for human rights didn't disappear—Congress, which controlled the aid purse strings, required the administration to certify that repressive regimes were making progress in this area before aid was increased.) High on the list was El Salvador, where U.S. backing helped a moderate elected government come to power in 1984. The new president, José Napoleón Duarte, moved against right-wing "death squads" that had been responsible for a number of kidnappings and murders and began talks with the leftist rebels. But he was unable to bring peace to the country. In fact, as the fighting continued, left and right became increasingly polarized, each intent on gaining exclusive control.

Support for the Contras ›

In Nicaragua, the Reagan administration tried a tactic the United States had used before in Central America: It backed a force of rebels in an attempt to destabilize the leftist government. The rebels, who became known as the contras, were a loose-knit group that included former supporters of Somoza, members of the Nicaraguan middle ground, and even some disenchanted former Sandinistas. The aid began secretly but soon became one of the most hotly debated policies of the Reagan years.

The administration first said that the goal of the contra operation was to pressure the Sandinistas into halting the supply of arms to the Salvadoran rebels and making democratic reforms. It soon became apparent, however, that the contras' goal was the overthrow of the Sandinista government. Reagan referred to them as "freedom fighters" and compared them to the Founding Fathers of the United States. Opponents of the aid said that the United States had no business fomenting civil war in a foreign country and asked how the administration could demand that Nicaragua stop aiding the Salvadoran rebels when the United States itself was aiding rebels in Nicaragua.

Among the actions the U.S. government took in support of the rebels was to aid in placing mines in Nicaraguan coastal waters. The goal was to block the flow of arms from Cuba to the Sandinistas and, through them, to the Salvadoran rebels. When the mining came to light, it brought a chorus of condemnation and a demand from the World Court, in May 1984, that it be stopped. The United States denied that it had violated international law, but it said that the mining had been stopped and would not be resumed.

By this time, public opinion had begun to swing against increased aid to the contras. People in the United States were still leery of becoming involved in another Vietnam. In mid-1984, Congress voted to bar further military aid to the rebel group. But aid did not stop—it simply went underground. In a startling admission late in 1986, the administration acknowledged that a small group of White House officials had taken the matter of contra aid into their own hands and developed a bizarre plan to keep the aid flowing. In violation of an embargo that had been in place since 1980, the group sold U.S. weapons to Iran (they hoped that, in exchange, Iran would secure the release of American hostages being held by Muslim terrorists in the Middle East). Then, through a tangled network of bogus corporations and Swiss bank accounts, the group diverted some of the profits from the sales to the contras.

After initial denials, Reagan admitted that he had approved the arms sales but denied knowledge of the diversion of profits to the contras. The officials involved—among them National Security Adviser Robert McFarlane; his successor, Vice Admiral John M. Poindexter; and their assistant Oliver North, a marine lieutenant colonel—had developed that phase of the plan on their own, Reagan said. Since most records of the transactions had been destroyed and others were highly classified, many details of the Iran-contra affair, as the scheme became known, remained shrouded in secrecy. But it raised broad questions about the conduct of U.S. foreign policy in general. And the revelation of the affair seemed to deal a final blow to the idea of contra aid. Although Congress had lifted the formal ban not long before the affair came to light, and although the administration continued to ask for aid, the idea found few backers.

While the United States was involved in the contra movement, Latin American countries were taking steps of their own to end the conflicts in Central America. The Contadora countries—a group that included Mexico, Venezuela, Panama, and Colombia—attempted to draw up a regional peace agreement, but both the United States and Nicaragua found problems with various drafts. Then, in 1987, five Central American countries agreed to a peace plan, called the Esquipulas agreement, worked out by Costa Rican president Oscar Arias Sánchez (Arias won the 1987 Nobel Peace Prize for his efforts). Under its terms, Nicaragua, Guatemala, Honduras, and El Salvador agreed to negotiate cease-fires with rebel groups, halt aid to insurgencies in other countries, and take steps to increase democracy. (Costa Rica, the fifth signer, was relatively untroubled by the conflicts that plagued the rest of the region. But its location south of Nicaragua had made it a staging ground for the contras.)

The United States was critical of the plan, largely because it provided no method of ensuring that the signers carried out their promises. In fact, several of the countries were slow to put the terms of the treaty into effect. The Sandinista government declared a cease-fire with the contras in 1988, but rather than taking steps toward democracy, it cracked down on its political opponents. In El Salvador, talks between the government and the rebels broke down, and killings by both right- and left-wing groups increased. Honduras and Guatemala also seemed to move slowly. But the U.S. position was also criticized, as undercutting the peace effort.

Drugs and Debt ›

By the end of the Reagan years, other Latin American problems had begun to loom larger in importance. As in the Carter years, immigration and, increasingly, drug trafficking continued to be thorny issues. The United States pressed Latin American countries to take stronger action against drugs. Latin Americans pointed out that as long as the United States did not control the enormous demand for drugs within its own borders, the illegal trade would likely continue. The export of cocaine and other drugs was a major (if illegal) factor in the economies of Colombia and several other countries. In some cases, high government officials were involved.

When steps were taken to control the drug trade, they often failed—as they did dramatically in Panama in 1988. There, after Panamanian General Manuel Noriega was indicted on drug-trafficking charges by a U.S. court, the United States attempted to use economic sanctions to force him to resign. The policy succeeded only in decimating Panama's economy; Noriega remained as the most powerful figure in the country.

Meanwhile, the issue of debt emerged to take center stage in U.S.–Latin American relations. Through the 1970s, many Latin American countries were financing their economic development with enormous borrowing from abroad. Mexico was a case in point. In the flush of the 1970s oil boom, the country had built its foreign debt up to $80 billion, confident that its oil exports would allow it to pay off the burden. By 1982, Brazil, banking on its rapidly diversifying and expanding industries, had borrowed $87 billion; Argentina, $43 billion; Venezuela, $28 billion. Then came a crash in oil prices, a jump in interest rates, and a worldwide recession that sharply reduced these countries' incomes, forcing a number of them to suspend payments and refinance their debts.

Although new loans were worked out and a disaster was averted, the events sent a shudder through the international financial community. If Latin American and other developing countries truly defaulted on their debts, the result seemed likely to be an international financial crash. Yet for the debtor countries, the situation was increasingly difficult—just paying interest on the loans absorbed more and more of their output. Debt relief moved high on the list of their concerns.

A plan developed by U.S. Treasury Secretary James Baker in 1985 focused on free-market forces, in keeping with the Reagan administration's economic philosophy. Under this plan, loans would continue with easier repayment terms. In exchange, Latin American countries would change their economic policies to encourage the growth of private industry. For example, they would hand over state-run businesses to private owners. This in turn was supposed to encourage foreign firms and banks to invest in the countries. But the plan was largely unsuccessful. To many Latin Americans, it smacked of political interference. Private banks and investors, meanwhile, were not sold on the concept and began to reduce rather than increase their stake in the region.

By the end of the Reagan administration, Latin American debt had reached astounding proportions: Brazil owed $120 billion; Mexico, $107 billion; Argentina, $59 billion. According to World Bank figures for the major nations of the region, debt payments absorbed anywhere from 17 percent to 44 percent of export earnings. The debt thus had the effect of crippling economic growth, and a number of countries were gripped by runaway inflation in which prices were increasing several hundred percent a year. As the economic situation worsened, political dissatisfaction and unrest increased.

Early in 1989, a report by the Inter-American Dialogue (a panel of private experts drawn from throughout the Western hemisphere) sharply criticized the handling of the Latin American debt crisis. The group called on the United States and other developed countries to restructure the enormous debt and to increase capital investment in Latin America to stimulate growth. It also called for new development strategies on the part of Latin American countries and for new loans from international financial institutions. It called on the United States, which had amassed an enormous foreign debt of its own in the 1980s, to put its own economic house in order.

Perhaps most significantly, the report warned of the ultimate threat posed by the debt crisis: a descent into political turmoil and a return to repressive rule. According to the report, "As governments lose credibility and authority, the appeal of extremist solutions is rising and it becomes harder to institute the economic measures needed for recovery and growth. Latin America may be condemned to a long period of economic hardship and political turbulence, which may force civilian authorities to yield to military rule in some places."[1]

As George Bush took office as president in January 1989, he faced calls for a new approach to Latin American policy. Throughout the region, the situation seemed grim. Land reform remained a rarity in most countries; in fact, through the 1970s and 1980s, the trend had been for private landholdings to grow larger. Latin Americans were on the average poorer at the end of the decade than they had been in 1980. And the political repercussions of this were beginning to be seen. As the standard of living fell in countries that had made the transition to democracy, people began to associate democracy with hard times—and to become disenchanted with the system.

These were some of the immediate problems Bush faced in forming a Latin American policy:

› In Brazil, where the debt burden strained the economy to the breaking point, the annual inflation rate hit 933 percent in 1988. The effect on the average worker was decimating—a paycheck worth $100 at the beginning of a month would be worth only $34 at the end of that month. This made it impossible to plan or to even hope of getting ahead. Inflation threatened to be even higher in 1989, prompting the government to freeze wages and prices. Meanwhile, the country was attempting to continue its gradual transition to democracy and had scheduled its first popular vote for the presidency since 1960. As the standard of living eroded and hopelessness increased in the vast slums of São Paulo and Rio de Janeiro, leftist parties made strong gains in municipal elections. President José Sarney warned that the country faced a socialist revolution; others feared that the military would step in to reassert its control.

› In Peru, a reformist government headed by President Alan García Pérez had failed to quell a growing economic crisis or to halt attacks by the Shining Path guerrillas, a Maoist group that had been carrying on one of the region's bloodiest insurgencies since the beginning of the decade. García had been elected in 1985 and had moved quickly to suspend most of the interest payments on Peru's foreign debt, expecting that the economy would receive a shot in the arm as a result of keeping this money at home. But instead of expanding, the economy began to shrink, and inflation grew until prices were doubling every three months. Now García's term was drawing to a close, and the country's future course was unclear.

› In Colombia, one of Latin America's oldest democracies, political violence was on the rise; and drug traffickers virtually controlled Medellín, the country's second largest city. Here and elsewhere in Latin America, U.S.–backed drug control programs had largely failed. Agents were openly shot. Concern about possible environmental damage led Latin American countries to balk at a U.S. proposal to spray coca crops with a chemical herbicide.

› Panama was an economic disaster—even basic services such as city trash collection and traffic lights had stopped. Noriega was almost universally unpopular, but his grip on the military was such that opposition groups saw little hope of ousting him peacefully. It was widely expected that he would attempt to control presidential elections scheduled for May 1989.

› In El Salvador, eight years of government by moderates and massive U.S. aid had failed to bring an end to the civil war. In fact, the situation was deteriorating, with leftist rebels stepping up their attacks, right-wing death squads reappearing, and the constant fighting disrupting the economy. The government had made some progress in land reform and other areas, but was resisted at every turn by both right and left. A popular program to bring economic help to villages, for example, was thwarted when rebels began to murder village mayors. Meanwhile, President Duarte had become fatally ill, and in any case his term was set to end in June 1989. The general increase in rebel violence, mostly directed against civilians, led many people to support the right as being the group best able to restore order to the country, despite its appalling record of human rights violations. Thus, it was considered likely that the right wing would win the upcoming presidential election.

These government workers in Panama City prepare bags of groceries in March 1988 for the 130,000 public-sector workers who have not been paid due to the collapse of the Panamanian economy.

› Nicaragua faced an economic crisis, with an astounding inflation rate that topped 5,000 percent. How much of the crisis resulted from U.S. restrictions on trade and how much from the Sandinistas' restrictions on free enterprise was debated. Meanwhile, the Arias plan for peace in Central America appeared to have bogged down.

These countries were not alone in facing difficulties. For example, with oil revenues down, Venezuela, Mexico, and Ecuador faced growing economic problems and unrest. And the flood of immigrants from throughout Central America to the United States increased as people sought to escape bitter poverty and political upheaval.

The transition to a new U.S. administration touched off broad questions about U.S.–Latin American policy. To what degree should the United States intervene in Latin American affairs, diplomatically or militarily? Should it throw its support to regional efforts such as the Arias peace plan, or should it continue the sort of unilateral actions represented by the contras in Nicaragua? Should aid to the region increase, and how should aid be directed? Should Latin American countries be relieved of debt burdens that threatened to crush them? If so, who should ultimately take on these burdens—the banks, international agencies, American taxpayers?

How Bush would deal with the Latin American problems was not immediately clear. As Reagan's vice-president, he had backed the Reagan administration's policies, including aid to the contras. As a candidate for president, he indicated that he would not turn away from those policies. But there were signs that Bush might chart a somewhat different course. For example, his aides acknowledged that the idea of aid to the contras was dead—both Congress and public opinion were against it—and that the new president's policies would be likely to focus on diplomatic rather than military initiatives. Even before he took office, he called for a fresh look at the international debt problem. As a way of underscoring the importance of Latin America in U.S. policy, he sent Vice-President Dan Quayle to Venezuela and El Salvador in the first foreign trip by a high-ranking member of the new administration.

Yet whatever course Bush chose seemed likely to be difficult. Even these initial moves led to some misunderstanding and resentment. The call for a "fresh look" at the debt crisis, for example, was interpreted by many Latin Americans as a willingness to forgive the debt burden, but that was a course the Bush administration ruled out. Some Latin Americans also found Quayle's visit insulting, noting that he lacked credibility in his own country. Adding to the misunderstanding was the fact that during the 1988 campaign, Quayle had asserted that the Monroe Doctrine was "alive and well" and formed the basis of U.S. policy in the hemisphere, despite the fact that the doctrine had been repudiated half a century earlier and had not been invoked since that time.[1]

Moreover, the new U.S. administration was slow to develop a coherent Latin American policy of its own. It was months before a new undersecretary of state for Latin America was appointed. This meant that there was no single individual to coordinate U.S. regional policy, iron out the spe-

*Vice-President Dan Quayle embraces
newly inaugurated Venezuelan
president Carlos Andrés Pérez in Caracas.*

cifics, or deal directly with Latin American concerns. However, the Bush administration adopted a more cooperative approach than that of the Reagan administration. It worked out a compromise with Congress, under which the contras would continue to receive humanitarian but not military aid until early 1990.

Meanwhile, there were new developments in the region. The most notable of these sprang from meetings of the five signers of the Arias peace plan for Central America. The signers agreed to a plan to disarm and disband the contras. Most of the rebels were in Honduras; under U.N. and OAS supervision, they were to return peacefully to Nicaragua or depart for third countries (presumably the United States). In exchange, Nicaragua agreed to hold elections in February 1990, with international observers present to guarantee fairness. The country was also to guarantee press freedom and free some 1,600 political prisoners.

The agreement underscored the fact that the United States had lost the initiative in the region—Central American countries were prepared to go it alone.

As before, there were few enforcement measures in the agreement—no "or else" to require Nicaraguan elections or press freedom, for example. The United States objected to the plan on that ground, noting that Nicaragua had made and broken such promises before. But some analysts observed that Nicaragua's economic crisis itself might serve as an enforcement measure—the country could no longer hope to survive unless its relations with its neighbors improved and trade increased. Where the contras were concerned, the accord seemed mainly a recognition of the inevitable: With Honduras increasingly unwilling to serve as their host, and U.S. funding virtually nonexistent, their cause seemed hopeless.

There were new developments on the question of debt as well. Here, too, it seemed likely that Latin American countries would seize the initiative. The new president of Venezuela, Carlos Andrés Pérez, urged that Latin American debtor nations act together to bargain with their creditors. Pérez advocated the creation of a special international agency that would buy back loans (that is, take them over and refinance them at lower rates). Politicians who shared his views on debt relief were gaining support in Argentina and Brazil. The United States was leery of the plan because it placed more of the burden on governments (and taxpayers) than on private banks. It advanced a new debt plan of its own that, like the Baker plan, emphasized the growth of private business. But the new plan also accepted the need for banks and international lending agencies to reduce debt payments and refinance more of the loans at lower interest rates. The U.S. plan was adopted by the International Monetary Fund and the World Bank in April 1989.

The Bush administration soon faced other policy decisions in Latin America. As many observers had predicted, the far-right ARENA party came to power in El Salvador's March election, raising fears of increased violence and human rights abuses. The United States adopted a wait-and-see approach. Panama's election in May produced an even more disastrous outcome. Although Noriega's opponents won by a landslide, the general first attempted to steal the election by fraud and then simply nullified the results. Opposition leaders who led street demonstrations were severely beaten.

The events in Panama placed the United States in a difficult position. Some people (including some Panamanians) called on the United States to send in troops and oust the general. Others warned that such an action would be seen as self-interested intervention—or even an attempt to break the Canal treaties. Bush hinted broadly that a coup would be welcome, but initially he called on the OAS to negotiate a settlement. When this effort failed, the United States lent support (but not combat troops) to a coup attempt by Panamanian military officers. The attempt failed, resulting in a major embarrassment for the United States. Still, some observers noted that Noriega's support was so low, even in the military, that his downfall seemed inevitable. U.S. officials did not rule out the possibility of another coup attempt.

The Policy Debate ›

To many observers, the 1989 questions over U.S. policy formed just the latest chapter in a long-running and much broader debate. The United States has frequently been accused of acting out of self-interest in Latin America. Economically, some critics of U.S. policy say, American aid has often worked against economic development that might threaten U.S. business interests. Politically, the United States has supported authoritarian dictatorships even when they were accused of torture and murder. The United States has been charged with backing Latin American democracy only when it is in its interests to do so. For example, critics charge, the United States withdrew its support for Somoza only when his regime was tottering and its downfall seemed certain.

To these objections, critics of the Reagan administration added that its policies were simplistic and outdated. By devoting most of its attention to a search for a Communist behind every bush, some analysts said, the United States failed to see the realities of modern Latin America: its growing role in world politics and the mounting economic problems that underlie its social unrest. By viewing all movement toward change as a movement toward Communism, the United States often thwarted reforms that might have helped correct those problems.

But other analysts argue that U.S. aid has brought many benefits to Latin America, and that where it has failed, this has often been more the result of waste, mismanagement, and sometimes corruption on the receiving end than of misguided U.S. policies. The trend toward democracy in Latin America during the late 1970s and 1980s is, they say, at least partly a result of U.S. efforts. As for the charge of U.S. self-interest, they add, it would be a strange foreign policy indeed that did not seek to further the interests of the nation. In short, the question is not whether the United States should advance its interests in Latin America, but how those interests can best be advanced.

Latin America's social and political problems are not simply the result of U.S. meddling, they add. These problems stem from social structures and cultural attitudes that were in place long before the United States had any impact on the region. In this view, the U.S. impact on Latin America has been overstated—the United States makes a convenient scapegoat for economic and political turmoil, so it is blamed for sending too little aid here or too much there, for intervening in one situation or failing to take action in another.

The fact remains that past U.S. actions in Latin America have often backfired, as we have seen. Even when they have been judged successful, these actions have frequently had the long-term effect of increasing resentment of the United States. But Latin Americans themselves have often been ambivalent about their relations with the United States, sometimes resentful of U.S. interference and sometimes welcoming economic and political support. Many Latin Americans believe that the United States, as a rich country, has an obligation to help their region economically, but they object to aid that comes with strings attached.

In reality, the problems in the region are complex, and the solutions will not be simple. Throughout the region, the transformation from agricultural to industrial society is continuing even as economic difficulties mount. But the transformation has not brought changes throughout society to the degree that the Industrial Revolution did in Europe and North America. Like many of Latin America's problems, this one is rooted in the past, in the social structure that keeps the elite in place and in other ways. For example, the Peruvian writer Hernando de Soto, in his 1989 book *The Other Path*, put forth another possible explanation for the region's continuing economic troubles. From Spain, Peru (and many other Latin American countries) inherited a top-heavy mercantilist tradition—that is, a tendency for heavy government regulation and control. Because of the tangle of red tape involved in setting up a legitimate business, many people make their living in various black market and "informal" enterprises. But because they operate outside the law, they cannot expand their businesses—they can't get financing, and if they grow too large, they will invite government action. Thus the economy as a whole is held back.

Today there seems to be a growing consensus that only broad and basic changes in the region's social and economic structure—spreading wealth and power more evenly through society—can end the vicious cycle of poverty, unrest, and repression. There is a crying need for creative solutions, particularly where debt is concerned.

What role should the United States play? Modern communications have made both politics and economics global, not regional, affairs. Gone are the days when a strong merchant navy could control a region's trade, as Britain's fleet controlled Latin America's in the early 1800s. Since the period after World War II, when the United States dominated not only Latin American trade but trade throughout the free world, new competition has emerged from the booming economies of Asia and Europe. Even defense concerns have changed—the Cuban missile crisis stemmed from the placement of Soviet nuclear weapons within easy striking distance of the United States, but today nuclear missiles can strike halfway around the world in thirty minutes.

These changes mean that the traditional concerns that have guided U.S. policy in Latin America—national security, economic advantage, the maintenance of a sphere of influence—need closer examination. The Soviet Union does not need to place missiles in Cuba to threaten the United States. In the face of increased competition worldwide, economically and politically, it seems unrealistic for the United States to expect to retain the dominance it enjoyed right after World War II. The debt crisis and other Latin American problems affect countries around the world, not only the United States.

Thus, solutions need to be worked out internationally. Above all, solutions need to recognize and deal with the concerns of Latin Americans. There is little security for the United States in the political upheavals that wrack Latin American countries, little advantage to be gained in economies that are spiraling out of control, and little influence to be won in an atmosphere of resentment and misunderstanding. Today the United States and Latin America are players on the world stage, competitors as well as partners. They have much to gain by working together—and much to lose by conflict.

SOURCE NOTES

Chapter Three

1. Quoted in Thomas A. Bailey, *A Diplomatic History of the American People* (New York: Appleton-Century-Crofts, 1958), p. 168.
2. Ibid., p. 178.
3. Quoted in *America: Great Crises in Our History Told by Its Makers*, Vol. 6 (Chicago: 1925), pp. 293–94.
4. Bailey, p. 187.

Chapter Four

1. Quoted in E. Bradford Burns, *Latin America: A Concise Interpretive History* (Englewood Cliffs, N.J.: Prentice-Hall, 1982), p. 156.
2. Ibid., p. 155.
3. Bailey, p. 454.
4. Hayes's remark came in a message to the Senate in March 1880; quoted in Bailey, p. 397.
5. Roosevelt's annual message to Congress, December 1904; quoted in James Petras, *Latin America: From Dependence to Revolution* (New York: John Wiley and Sons, 1973), p. 242.
6. Roosevelt to White, September 13, 1906; quoted in Bailey, p. 500.

Chapter Five

1. Bailey, p. 556.

Chapter Six

1. Petras, p. 256.

Chapter Seven

1. *New York Times*, January 17, 1989, p. 3.

Chapter Eight

1. *New York Times*, September 23, 1988, p. 23.

FOR FURTHER READING

The story of the United States and Latin America continues to unfold daily in the news media. In addition to current accounts, the following works may be helpful to readers who seek deeper knowledge of the subject.

E. Bradford Burns's *Latin America: A Concise Interpretive History* (Prentice-Hall, 1982) and Thomas E. Skidmore and Peter H. Smith's *Modern Latin America* (Oxford University Press, 1984) provide excellent accounts of the forces that have shaped Latin America. Skidmore and Smith, as their title suggests, place more emphasis on recent events, taking a close look at developments in Argentina, Brazil, Central America, Cuba, Mexico, and Peru. Thomas A. Bailey's *A Diplomatic History of the American People*, first published in 1940 (Appleton-Century-Crofts), often takes views that present-day analysts might find dated. But its highly readable, detailed accounts of the twists and turns of U.S. policy (and of the personalities behind it) are still valuable.

An in-depth view of U.S. relations with Latin America (and particularly with Mexico, Brazil, and the countries of the Caribbean Basin) is offered by Abraham F. Lowenthal in *Partners in Conflict: The United States and Latin America* (Johns Hopkins University Press, 1987). In *Latin America: From Dependence to Revolution* (John Wiley and Sons, 1973), James Petras includes a critical look at the Monroe Doctrine and the U.S. policies that followed it. A chilling link between U.S. policy and human rights abuses in Latin America is presented in *With Friends Like These: The Americas Watch Report on Human Rights and U.S. Policy in Latin America* (Cynthia Brown, editor; Pantheon, 1985).

As events in Latin America continue to unfold, so does the U.S. policy debate. Many of the authors named above express clear opinions in one direction or another. A useful summary of some of the points in the debate, set out in terms that can be readily understood, can be found in *Latin America and U.S. Foreign Policy: Opposing Viewpoints* (Green Haven Press, 1988). U.S. intervention, human rights, revolution, and international debt are among the subjects taken on in essays collected from various sources.

INDEX

Ford, Gerald, 114
Foreign debt, 68–70, 73, 74,
    131–133, 139, 142, 147
France, 28, 49, 51, 64, 91
Franklin, Benjamin, 28
Free trade, 68
Frei, Eduardo, 107
French West Indies, 87

Gadsden Purchase, 50
García Pérez, Alan, 135
Garfield, James, 55
Germany, 85, 88–89, 93
Goliad, 48
Good Neighbor Policy, 84–85,
    87–88
Goulart, João, 107
Great Britain, 28, 36, 40, 41,
    43–46, 49, 51, 63–65, 91,
    126
Great Depression, 84, 88, 89,
    95
Grenada, 14, 123–126
Greytown, 63, 64
Guam, 62
Guatemala, 56, 76, 96–98, 118,
    126, 129, 130
Guevara, "Che," 105

Haciendas (ranches), 22
Haiti, 46, 57, 74, 76, 80, 81,
    85, 86, 100, 126
Harding, Warren G., 81
Harrison, William Henry, 55
Hayes, Rutherford B., 64
Hay-Pauncefote Treaty of
    1901, 65
Hidalgo y Costilla, Miguel,
    32, 34
Hispaniola, 57
Holy (Quintuple) Alliance,
    40–43

Honduras, 74, 76, 126, 129,
    130, 141, 142
Hoover, Herbert, 82–83
Houston, Sam, 47
Huerta, Victoriano, 77–79
Human rights, 4, 118–121,
    126, 136

Immigration, 13, 117–118, 130
Incas, 18, 27
Industry, 27, 68, 75, 88, 94,
    95, 112
Inflation, 132, 135, 138
Inquisition, 26
Inter-American Development
    Commission, 88
Inter-American Dialogue,
    132–133
International Monetary Fund,
    142
Investment, 13, 59, 71, 74,
    77–80, 95
Iran-contra affair, 128–129
Isabella, Queen, 22
Iturbide, Agustín de, 33, 34

Jackson, Andrew, 39, 46, 48
Jefferson, Thomas, 28
Jesuits, 29
João VI, Dom, 29
Johnson, Lyndon B., 108
Joseph Bonaparte, 30
Juárez, Benito, 51

Kennedy, John F., 102–103,
    105
Kissinger, Henry, 114
Korean War, 94

Land reform, 34, 77, 80, 94,
    120, 134
Language, 17

Reagan, Ronald, 122–130, 132, 138–139, 141, 144
Rio Pact of 1947, 93–94
Rockefeller, Nelson, 109
Rockefeller report, 109, 111
Roman Catholic Church, 25–27, 29
Roosevelt, Franklin Delano, 84–85, 87, 89, 93
Roosevelt, Theodore, 55, 65, 68–71, 125
Roosevelt Corollary, 69
Rousseau, Jean-Jacques, 28
Russia, 41, 42

Sandinistas, 119–120, 127–130
Sandino, Augusto César, 81, 82, 119
San Jacinto, battle of, 48
San Martin, José de, 31, 32, 34
Santa Anna, Antonio López de, 47–48
Santo Domingo, 51, 80, 81
Sarney, José, 135
Seward, William H., 59
Slavery, 23, 47, 48, 58
Smith, Adam, 28
Smoot-Hawley Tariff Act, 84, 88
Somoza Debayle, Anastasio, 119, 144
Somoza García, Anastasio, 81–82, 119
Soviet Union, 14, 92–95, 100, 103, 105, 114, 123, 125–126, 146, 147
Spain, 17–18, 20–33, 36, 37, 39–42, 51, 58–61, 87, 145
Spanish-American War, 60, 62

Stalin, Joseph, 92
Strong, Josiah, 54

Taft, William Howard, 55, 71, 74
Tampico incident, 78–79
Texas, 46–50
Torrijos, Omar, 116
Trade, 13, 14, 26, 29, 30, 41, 55–57, 68, 81, 84, 88, 112, 122
Treaty of Ghent, 36
Trujillo, Rafael, 108
Truman, Harry S., 93, 94

United Fruit Company, 74, 96
Uruguay, 46, 93, 126

Van Buren, Martin, 49
Venezuela, 25, 30–32, 36, 69, 105, 114, 129, 131, 138, 142
Veracruz, 46, 79
Vietnam, 111, 114
Villa, Francisco, 78, 79
Virgin Islands, 59, 80

War of 1812, 36
Watergate scandal, 114
Wilson, Woodrow, 76–81, 84, 121
World Bank, 132, 142
World Court, 128
World War I, 80–81
World War II, 85, 87–89, 93

Yucatán Peninsula, 50

Zelaya, José, 73

ABOUT THE AUTHOR

Elaine Pascoe is a free-lance writer and journalist whose articles have appeared in a number of national publications. She is the author of *South Africa: Troubled Land* and *Racial Prejudice* (in Franklin Watts's Issues in American History series), which was named an "outstanding trade book" by the National Council for the Social Studies and received a certificate of outstanding merit in the competition for the NCSS's Carter G. Woodson Award.